Arnulfo L. Oliveira Memorial Library

Finding Jefferson: A Lost Letter, A Remarkable Discovery,
and the First Amendment in an Age of Terrorism
Blasphemy: How the Religious Right Is Hijacking the Declaration
of Independence
Preemption: A Knife That Cuts Both Ways
What Israel Means to Me
Rights from Wrongs: A Secular Theory of the Origins of Rights
America on Trial
The Case for Peace
The Case for Israel
America Declares Independence
Why Terrorism Works
Shouting Fire
Letters to a Young Lawyer
Supreme Injustice
Genesis of Justice
Just Revenge
Sexual McCarthyism
The Vanishing American Jew
Reasonable Doubts
The Abuse Excuse
The Advocate's Devil
Contrary to Popular Opinion
Chutzpah
Taking Liberties
Reversal of Fortune
Best Defense
Criminal Law: Theory and Process
Psychoanalysis, Psychiatry and Law

IS THERE A RIGHT TO REMAIN SILENT?

INALIENABLE RIGHTS SERIES

. . .

Is There a Right to Remain Silent?

. . .

COERCIVE INTERROGATION AND

THE FIFTH AMENDMENT AFTER 9/11

Alan M. Dershowitz

OXFORD
UNIVERSITY PRESS
2008

OXFORD
UNIVERSITY PRESS

Oxford University Press, Inc., publishes works that further
Oxford University's objective of excellence
in research, scholarship, and education.

Oxford   New York
Auckland   Cape Town   Dar es Salaam   Hong Kong   Karachi
Kuala Lumpur   Madrid   Melbourne   Mexico City   Nairobi
New Delhi   Shanghai   Taipei   Toronto

With offices in
Argentina   Austria   Brazil   Chile   Czech Republic   France   Greece
Guatemala   Hungary   Italy   Japan   Poland   Portugal   Singapore
South Korea   Switzerland   Thailand   Turkey   Ukraine   Vietnam

Copyright © 2008 by Alan M. Dershowitz

Published by Oxford University Press, Inc.
198 Madison Avenue, New York, New York 10016

www.oup.com

Oxford is a registered trademark of Oxford University Press

Library of Congress Cataloging-in-Publication Data
Dershowitz, Alan M.
Is there a right to remain silent? : coercive interrogation and the Fifth
Amendment after 9/11 / Alan M. Dershowitz.
p.   cm.—(Inalienable rights series)
ISBN 978-0-19-530779-5
1. Self-incrimination—United States.   2. United States. Constitution.
5th Amendment.   3. United States. Supreme Court.   4. Right to counsel—
United States.   5. Police questioning—United States.   6. Civil rights—
United States.   I. Title.
KF9668.D47 2008
345.73'056—dc22   2007043079

1 3 5 7 9 8 6 4 2

Printed in the United States of America
on acid-free paper

This book is dedicated to my great teachers at Brooklyn college who first stimulated my interest in constitutional law. Among them were professors John Hope Franklin, Elsa de Haas, John Hospers, Eric G. James, Samuel Konefsky, Martin Landau, Charles Parkhurst, Benjamin Rivlin, Madeline Russell Robinton, Georgia H. Wilson, and Belle Zeller. Half a century later, I still think about what they taught me. That is truly the mark of great teachers.

Acknowledgments

. . .

My student assistants do not have a right to remain silent. They are obliged to speak their minds and they do, with much appreciation. Among those who spoke their minds as well as helped with the research for this book were the following: Alexander Blenkinsopp, Aaron Voloj Dessauer, Charles Johnson, Chaim Kagedan, Nicholas Krasney, Curtis Leitner, Peter Mulcahy, and Jessica Tisch.

Contents

. . .

CONTENTS

Series Editor's Note

. . .

We hold these truths to be self-evident, that all men are created equal, that they are endowed by their Creator with certain unalienable Rights....

——THE DECLARATION OF INDEPENDENCE

. . .

THE "SELF-INCRIMINATION" CLAUSE of the Fifth Amendment provides: "No person shall be...compelled in any criminal case to be a witness against himself." Over the past half-century, the guarantee has entered the public consciousness as the "right to remain silent." In *Is There a Right to Remain Silent?*, Alan Dershowitz takes on the following question: Suppose government officials torture an individual in order to coerce him into revealing information that it will use, not in a criminal prosecution of the individual who is tortured, but to prevent possible future crimes, including future acts of terrorism. In such circumstances, has the government violated the individual's "right to remain silent"?

As Dershowitz explains, this is a critical question. As we move from a "reactive state," focused primarily on punishing individuals who have committed crimes, to a "preventive state," focused primarily on gathering information to enable the government to anticipate and prevent terrorist or other criminal acts, we must consider whether traditional constitutional rights should be reinterpreted to ensure they retain their vitality in a changing world.

In examining this issue, Dershowitz begins with the Supreme Court's 2003 decision in *Chavez v. Martinez*, in which a majority of the justices held that there was no violation of the "right to remain silent" when police officers employed brutal interrogation techniques against an individual, so long as the government did not use the information extracted from the individual in any criminal trial in which he was the accused. Put differently, the Court held that the Fifth Amendment right to remain silent is violated *only when the information is used against the individual in a criminal case.* The use of coercion, even coercion bordering on torture, to obtain information from an individual does not itself violate the right.

In *Is There a Right to Remain Silent?*, Dershowitz explores the text, history, purposes, and evolution of the Fifth Amendment guarantee in order to test both the persuasiveness of the Court's conclusion in *Chavez* and, more fundamentally, the very process of constitutional interpretation.

Dershowitz concedes that a literal reading of the text would seem to support such a narrow understanding of the clause. But he then demonstrates that such a literal reading would have made no sense even to the framers of the Fifth Amendment, because it would have rendered the guarantee almost a nullity. He considers the virtues and vice of "originalism" as a method of constitutional exegesis and demonstrates that the rigid application of such an approach is, at least in this context, largely self-contradictory and incoherent, incompatible with the intent of the framers both in terms of the purposes the clause was intended to serve and in terms of their understanding of a constitution, incompatible with the Court's construction and application of the clause over the past two centuries, and an unsound approach to constitutional interpretation in an ever-changing society.

But if simple "originalism" comes up empty, what is a court to do? Dershowitz reviews the deeper historical and religious roots of the clause to get a fuller sense of its purposes. He then considers those purposes, examines how the Court has attempted to construe the clause in order to achieve them, and explores the policy implications of various possible interpretations of the right to remain silent, particularly in light of the realities of the contemporary criminal justice system and the emergence of the preventive state.

Dershowitz demonstrates with real insight the magnitude of the quandary. How, he asks, "should an intellectually honest justice committed to nonideological interpretation of the Constitution go about construing" the privilege against self-incrimination when (a) the text is "subject to multiple, reasonable interpretations"; (b) the precedents "could sustain multiple plausible interpretations"; (c) analogies are "incomplete, flawed, or cut in multiple directions"; (d) the "original understanding leads to no single interpretation"; (e) the current system of criminal justice is profoundly different "from the various systems in place at the founding"; (f) the traditional understanding of the privilege, "especially its symbolic power," does not support "limiting it to a technical trial remedy available only to criminal defendants"; (g) more recent understandings of the clause "have varied with the climate of the times and the nature of the 'wrongs' "; (h) "functional consideration of constitutional policy cuts both ways depending on one's political, ideological, and other preferences";

and (i) various competing modes of constitutional interpretation "fail to produce a satisfactory singular result."

In addressing this dilemma, *Is There a Right to Remain Silent?* cuts to the very core of the challenge of constitutional law.

2008   Geoffrey R. Stone

Introduction

· · ·

"YOU HAVE THE RIGHT to remain silent." It's probably the best known phrase to emanate from our Constitution. Every school-child, movie-goer, and TV watcher knows that the Bill of Rights, most particularly the Fifth Amendment, grants every American the right to remain silent. The late chief justice William Rehnquist observed that the *Miranda* warnings—which begin with the categorical statement "You have the right to remain silent"—have "become part of our national culture." He was correct, as evidenced by one of the most reliable barometers of American culture, Jerry Seinfeld:

> "Aren't you a little surprised that cops still have to read that whole 'You have the right to remain silent' speech to every criminal they arrest? I mean is there anybody who doesn't know that by now? Can't they just go, 'Freeze, you're under arrest. You ever seen *Baretta*?'"

"'Yeah.'"

"'Good, get in the car.'"

Justice Scalia agreed with Seinfeld that "[i]n the modern age of frequently dramatized 'Miranda' warnings, [it] is implausible" that a "person under investigation may be unaware of his right to remain silent."

But do Americans actually have the right that police officers are constitutionally obliged to tell them they have? Not according to a recent Supreme Court decision, largely unnoticed not only by the general public but by the academy as well. In this relatively obscure lawsuit for monetary damages growing out of a rather routine, if disturbing, police interrogation, a majority of Supreme Court justices ruled that whatever the courts might have said and whatever most people might believe, Americans never did have a right to remain silent. And if perchance they ever did, they certainly don't have it now. This case, in which an interrogated suspect named Oliverio Martinez sued a police officer named Benjamin Chavez, can be seen as a bellwether for the rise of what I call "the preventive state," namely, a government that seeks to head off harmful conduct before it occurs, rather than waiting to punish such conduct—in order to deter others—until after it has taken place. Although the rise of the preventive state has been driven largely by the terrible events of 9/11, the *Martinez* case, properly understood, bears a close connection to post-9/11 terrorism policies, even though the case itself involved an ordinary crime. In that case, the Supreme Court—employing highly questionable interpretive mechanisms—told Americans, in effect, the following: "You may *believe* you have the right to remain silent. We may have *told you* that you have the right to remain silent. Policemen may have the *obligation to advise you* that you have the right to remain silent. But you *do not* have the right to remain silent. You do not even have the right not to be compelled or coerced into confessing your crimes. All you have is the right to *exclude* the fruits of compelled self-incrimination at your criminal trial—*if* you ever have a criminal trial. If the objective of the interrogation is to produce intelligence information rather than evidence to be used against you in your criminal trial—an increasingly common objective in the age of terrorism—you may have no constitutional rights at all."

There is a big difference between the fundamental *right* to remain silent and a narrow trial *remedy* limited to the exclusion of evidence. This difference is becoming increasingly important as coercive interrogation is used more frequently to obtain *information* deemed necessary to prevent *future* crimes (especially terrorism) than to secure *evidence* with which to prosecute *past* crimes. This may be part of a more general trend toward narrowing what many have long understood to be fundamental human rights—such as the presumption of innocence, the right to counsel, and the prohibition against cruel and unusual punishments—into limited trial and posttrial rights for criminal defendants. Taken together, these developments enhance the power of government at the expense of the individual when it is acting preventively, as distinguished from punitively. They threaten to leave a gaping "black hole" in our system of constitutional protections, as prevention takes on an increasingly important role, specifically in the war against terrorism and more generally in the preventive state.

We lack a general jurisprudence and constitutional law governing preventive intrusions designed to anticipate and head off future harms. As we move away from the old paradigm of the deterrent state—in which we wait until the crime is committed and then punish the offender in order to deter him and others—and toward the new paradigm of the preventive state, the old jurisprudence and constitutional law must be adapted to the new realities of seriously intrusive actions taken by government in the name of prevention rather than punishment.

We shall also explore the undemocratic implications of wide disparities between what citizens *believe* are their rights and what courts actually *enforce* as rights. What does it say about a nation when the majority of its citizens, even its most educated, understand an important constitutional protection so differently—and so much more broadly—than its courts do? And we shall consider the modalities by which the courts, especially the Supreme Court, interpret or expound the often ambiguous text of our Constitution, and its often inconclusive history, in an effort to reconcile conflicting precedents, expectations, analogies, and doctrines. Finally, we shall evaluate the policy considerations underlying this old right and try to apply them to the new realities of preventive intelligence-gathering in the age of terrorism.

IS THERE A RIGHT TO REMAIN SILENT?

CHAPTER ONE

. . .

What Is the Right against Self-Incrimination?

THE FIFTH AMENDMENT to the Constitution contains a hodge-podge of rights, some of which apply only to criminal defendants, whereas others have more general application. It is an example of Churchill's pudding with "no theme." The Fifth Amendment reads, in whole, as follows:

> No person shall be held to answer for a capital, or otherwise infamous crime, unless on a presentment or indictment of a Grand Jury, except in cases arising in the land or naval forces, or in the Militia, when in actual service in time of War or public danger; nor shall any person be subject for the same offense to be twice put in jeopardy of life or limb; nor shall be compelled in any criminal case to be a witness against himself, nor be deprived of life, liberty, or property, without due process of law; nor shall private property be taken for public use, without just compensation.

Notwithstanding its wide assortment of rights, the Fifth Amendment in common parlance has come to refer specifically to the provision that "no person...shall be compelled in any criminal case to be a witness against himself." Although it is called a "privilege," which suggests a revocable concession given by the government to its subjects, in the United States it is a constitutional right that imposes irrevocable limitations on the government.

Read literally and narrowly, this right would be limited to precluding prosecutors in a criminal case from compelling the defendant to testify, under oath, against himself at his own trial. That is the technical meaning of the words "witness against himself." Such a literal interpretation would have rendered the right virtually meaningless at the time it was written, since defendants were *disqualified* from testifying under oath—from being "witnesses"—at their own criminal trials whether they wanted to or not. Thus, even if there were no constitutional right not to be compelled to testify against oneself, no defendant could be compelled to do so at the time the Fifth Amendment became part of our Constitution. It is unlikely that the framers of the Fifth Amendment intended to include in the Bill of Rights a protection that had no applicability to the legal system as they knew it. Accordingly, despite its words, the right had never, until this recent decision, been interpreted in such a selectively literal manner.

In 1969, Professor Leonard Levy summarized the jurisprudence as follows: "Seeking the spirit and policy of the fifth, the [Supreme] Court has, on the whole, given it an ever-widening, liberal interpretation, on the principle that 'it is as broad as the mischief against which it seeks to guard.' " For example, shortly after it was ratified, the right was interpreted to apply to witnesses who *might become* criminal defendants, as well as to those who *already were* criminal defendants. In subsequent decisions, it was also held applicable to pretrial, out-of-court police interrogation of in-court suspects, and not only to in-court questioning, under oath, of defendants by prosecutors or judges.

As we shall see, the origin of the right grew out of three somewhat different evidentiary privileges, with different histories and current applications. There was the *defendant's* privilege, which precluded the prosecution from compelling a criminal defendant to be a witness at his own trial. There was the *witness's* privilege, which granted to any witness in any legal proceeding the right to refuse to answer specific questions that might tend to incriminate him in a subsequent criminal case, unless he was given immunity that was at least as extensive as his privilege. And there was the *suspect's* privilege, which prohibited the government from using involuntary statements that were elicited from the defendant by pretrial coercion. Taken together, these privileges and their several variations have been summarized by courts and commentators as bestowing "the right of a person to remain silent." This characterization makes the privilege somewhat greater than the sum of its parts. The Supreme Court's recent decision makes the privilege considerably smaller than the sum of its parts, and reduces it from an array of rights protecting all "persons" to a specific remedy, available only to criminal defendants.

When the right against self-incrimination was included in the Bill of Rights, it generated little controversy or debate. Yet in recent times, it has created a hailstorm of criticism, from academics, politicians, and the general public.

Levy has acknowledged that during the McCarthy period he himself "wondered why the Bill of Rights contained a provision that benefited criminals and enemies of the United States. I knew enough about those who framed and ratified the Bill of Rights to understand that they could not be dismissed as fools, starry-eyed idealists, or mushy liberals." Levy's curiosity led him to write the first scholarly book on the history of the Fifth Amendment.

I too became interested in the Fifth Amendment during the McCarthy era. I was in high school and then in college at the time, and so I did not write a book—merely a term paper. In it, I explored the history, policies, and applications of the privilege, especially in the context of legislative investigations, where many of the battles over the scope of the Fifth Amendment were then being fought. I pointed out that the privilege had "traversed many cycles" over the years and had been "adapted to changing times and needs," and concluded that though we "are considering the very same constitutional phrase, we are dealing with a completely new and hitherto unknown privilege." I now believe, with Ecclesiastes, that there is rarely anything "completely new" under the sun, but it is true that the right against self-incrimination has undergone frequent reinterpretation and redefinition as our legal and political systems have changed over time and as our nation has experienced abuses of different kinds. We are currently in the midst of another such period of reinterpretation and redefinition, as we confront the dangers of terrorism. The challenges we face in seeking to balance these dangers against the potential abuses of the preventive state are as daunting as any in our long history of adapting the Constitution to changing times and circumstances.

Recently a prominent judge told me that while he understood the history and policies underlying all of the other rights in our Constitution, he did not understand why a guilty defendant should have the right to refuse, without consequence, to answer relevant questions properly put to him by a government official. This judge is joined by many academics and ordinary citizens who wonder about this and other questions that are naturally raised by the somewhat unnatural right against self-incrimination.

THE DIFFERENT MEANINGS OF THE FIFTH

The Fifth Amendment's privilege against self-incrimination has been interpreted by courts and commentators to mean radically different things over the years. Here are some of the most common interpretations, from the broadest to the narrowest, as articulated over the years by Supreme Court justices, sometimes in the majority, sometimes in concurring or dissenting opinions.

1. The right to remain silent: "The Fifth Amendment guarantees...the right of a person to remain silent unless he chooses to speak in the unfettered exercise of his own will, and to suffer no penalty...for such silence." (1964)

2. The right to a private enclave into which the government may not pry: "The privilege against self-incrimination... reflects many of our fundamental values and most noble aspirations [including] our respect for the inviolability of the human personality and of the right of each individual to 'a private enclave where he may lead a private life.'" (1964)

3. The right not to be compelled to expose one's own guilt: "The essential and inherent cruelty of compelling a man to expose his own guilt is...plain to every person who gives the subject a moment's thought." (1896)

4. The right not to be degraded: "A sense of personal degradation in being compelled to incriminate one's self must create a feeling of abhorrence in the community." (1896)

5. The right not to be subjected to a "cruel trilemma": "Our unwillingness to subject those suspected of crime to the cruel trilemma of self-accusation, perjury or contempt..." (1964)

6. The right not to be coerced by the police into making an involuntary self-incriminating statement: "The ultimate test remains . . . the test of voluntariness. Is the confession the product of an essentially free and unconstrained choice by its maker? If it is, if he has willed to confess, it may be used against him. If it is not, if his will has been overborne and his capacity for self-determination critically impaired, the use of his confession offends due process." (1961)

7. The right to be advised of the *Miranda* rules: "Prior to any questioning, the person must be warned that he has a right to remain silent, that any statement he does make may be used as evidence against him, and that he has a right to the presence of an attorney, either retained or appointed." (1966)

8. The right of a criminal defendant not to testify and not to have a fact finder draw inference of guilt from his decision: "For comment on the refusal to testify is a remnant of the inquisitorial system of criminal justice, which the Fifth Amendment outlaws. It is a penalty imposed by courts for exercising a constitutional privilege. It cuts down on the privilege by making its assertion costly." (1965)

9. The right to have prosecution bear heavy burden of proving defendant's guilt without relying on defendant's testimony (or lack thereof): "Requiring the government in its contest with the individual to shoulder the entire load . . . " (1964)

   "The privilege against self-incrimination [is] the essential mainstay of our adversary system." (1966)

10. The right not to be tortured into providing incriminating information: "[The Fifth Amendment] protects all citi-

zens from the kind of custodial interrogation that was once employed by the Star Chamber, by 'the Germans of the 1930's and early 1940's,' and by some of our own police departments only a few decades ago." (1985)

11. The right to enjoin or seek damages against government officials who violate these rights: "The police may not prolong or increase a suspect's suffering against the suspect's will. In [such] a case ... recovery should be available under § 1983 if a complainant can demonstrate that an officer exploited his pain and suffering with the purpose and intent of securing an incriminating statement." (2003, dissenting opinion of Justice Kennedy in *Chavez v. Martinez*)

12. The right only to exclude self-incriminating statements and their fruits from any use in criminal prosecution against the defendant: "Statements compelled by police interrogations ... may not be used against a defendant at trial ... but it is not until their use in a criminal case that a violation of the *Self-Incrimination* Clause occurs." (2003)

13. The right to exclude self-incriminating statements obtained in violation of *Miranda*, but not its fruits, from the government's case in chief against the defendant, and not even the statement if the defendant takes the stand: "Failure to give a suspect the warnings prescribed by *Miranda v. Arizona* [does not require] suppression of the physical fruits of the suspect's unwarned but voluntary statements." (2003)

"The shield provided by *Miranda* cannot be perverted into a license to use perjury by way of a defense, free from the risk of confrontation with prior inconsistent [un-Mirandized] utterances." (1971)

These are but a few of the formulations of the Fifth Amendment rendered by the justices. As we shall see, the scope and application of the right against self-incrimination have varied over time with the intensity of governmental efforts and the means employed to elicit information from individuals.

· · ·

CHAPTER TWO

The Supreme Court's Recent Decision

CHAVEZ V. MARTINEZ, decided on May 27, 2003, was a civil, not a criminal, case, but it decided an important constitutional issue regarding the meaning and scope of the right against self-incrimination. The victim of police coercion sued the police officer under a federal statute. The law grants a police officer "qualified immunity" from such a lawsuit unless his conduct violated a constitutional right. It was necessary, therefore, for the Supreme Court to determine whether the officer had violated the victim's constitutional right.

The lower courts ruled that the police officer had violated the plaintiff's constitutional rights by subjecting him to coercive interrogation after he had been shot by another officer. As a result of this coercion, the plaintiff made statements that were self-incriminating. He admitted that he pointed a gun at a police officer before he was shot by another officer. The plaintiff was never charged with any crime, and his coerced self-incriminating statements were never used against him in a criminal prosecution. The Supreme Court granted review to decide whether police coercion alone, without the subsequent use of the fruits of such coercion against the person in a criminal case, violated the Fifth Amendment.

There were six opinions, none of which alone represented the majority view, but the opinion of Justice Thomas, joined by Chief Justice Rehnquist and Justices O'Connor and Scalia, carried the day and is likely to reflect the views of a majority of the current Court. That opinion concluded that Martinez's privilege against self-incrimination had not been violated by police officers who had coerced him into making statements that were self-incriminating because the statements were never *used against him* in a criminal case. Justice Souter "concurred" in the Court's judgment that mere compulsion does not violate the privilege against self-incrimination so long as the resulting "testimony" is not admitted into evidence at the person's criminal trial. Justice Breyer joined Souter's opinion.

Three justices—Stevens, Kennedy, and Ginsburg—concluded, in dissent, that the privilege could be violated whenever "torture or its close equivalents are brought to bear" on a person, regardless of whether the fruits of the interrogation are ultimately admitted against him in a criminal case. Not a single justice accepted the view that the mere use of coercion that would be sufficient to exclude a statement from a criminal trial but that is short of "torture or its close equivalent" would constitute a stand-alone violation of the privilege, absent subsequent use of the statement.

The nose count therefore was 6–3 on the fundamental constitutional issue of whether the privilege against self-incrimination bestows any right to remain silent. The majority said no. Nor does the privilege grant a correlative right not to be compelled or coerced into making statements that are self-incriminating. The only right granted by the Fifth Amendment is a criminal *trial* remedy, and all it requires is that *if* compulsion has been employed against a person by government officials—police or judges—the resulting statements (and their fruits) may not be *admitted into evidence* against that person at a subsequent criminal trial, if there ever is one.

Absent such *use* of coerced statements, there has been no violation of the privilege, no matter how extreme the coercion. Even the three dissenters would require more than a mere violation of a citizen's right to remain silent, or his right not to be coerced into making incriminating statements, for there to be a violation of the privilege. According to the Stevens standard, unless the government employed "torture or its close equivalents," there would be no violation of the privilege. All nine justices rejected the widespread belief that the Fifth Amendment bestows on all Americans the right to remain silent, even in the face of coercive questions, and that the use of coercion by the police violates the right against self-incrimination.

Justice Souter's opinion ended with a one-sentence conclusion remanding the case for a determination of whether Martinez "may pursue a claim of liability for a substantive due process violation." This final paragraph constituted "the opinion of the Court." In other words, a majority of the Court, while deciding that coercion does not violate *the privilege against self-incrimination*, left open the question of whether the coercion at issue in this case rose to the level of a substantive *due process* violation. Justices Thomas, Scalia, Rehnquist, and O'Connor voted against the remand, being "satisfied that [the interrogation in this case, though coercive,] did not violate Martinez's due process rights." According to these four justices, there was nothing unconstitutional about an interrogation that Justice Stevens characterized as "the functional equivalent of... torturous methods."

What, then, were these methods? The facts of the case were essentially undisputed, because the crucial moments of the interrogation were captured on tape. Here are the facts as set out, somewhat antiseptically, by Justice Thomas. He begins by describing what happened after Martinez's arrest:

> [Officer Salinas] conducted a patdown frisk and discovered a knife in Martinez's waistband. An altercation ensued....
>
> The officers claim that Martinez drew Salinas' gun from its holster and pointed it at them; Martinez denies this. Both sides agree, however, that Salinas yelled, "He's got my gun!" Peña then drew her gun and shot Martinez several times, causing severe injuries that left Martinez permanently blinded and paralyzed from the waist down.

Justice Thomas then proceeds to describe the interrogation:

> Petitioner Chavez, a patrol supervisor...accompanied Martinez to the hospital and then questioned Martinez there while he was receiving treatment from medical personnel. The interview lasted a total of about 10 minutes, over a 45-minute period, with Chavez leaving the emergency room for periods of time to permit medical personnel to attend to Martinez.
>
> At first, most of Martinez's answers consisted of "I don't know," "I am dying," and "I am choking." Later in the interview, Martinez admitted that he took the gun from the officer's holster and pointed it at the police. He also admitted that he used heroin regularly. At one point, Martinez said "I am not telling you anything until they treat me," yet Chavez continued the interview. At no point during the interview was Martinez given warnings under *Miranda* v. *Arizona*.

THE SUPREME COURT'S RECENT DECISION

Justice Stevens provides a more graphic description, quoting the English translation of the tape-recorded questioning in Spanish that occurred in the emergency room of the hospital:

CHAVEZ: What happened? Oliverio, tell me what happened.

O[LIVERIO] M[ARTINEZ]: I don't know.

CHAVEZ: I don't know what happened [*sic*]?

O. M.: Ay! I am dying. Ay! What are you doing to me? No...! (Unintelligible scream).

CHAVEZ: What happened, sir?

O. M.: My foot hurts...

CHAVEZ: Oliverio. Sir, what happened?

O. M.: I am choking.

CHAVEZ: Tell me what happened.

O. M.: I don't know.

CHAVEZ: "I don't know."

O. M.: My leg hurts.

CHAVEZ: I don't know what happened [*sic*]?

O. M.: It hurts...

CHAVEZ: Hey, hey look.

O. M.: I am choking.

CHAVEZ: Can you hear? Look, listen, I am Benjamin Chavez with the police here in Oxnard, look.

O. M.: I am dying, please.

CHAVEZ: OK, yes, tell me what happened. If you are going to die, tell me what happened. Look I need to tell [*sic*] what happened.

O. M.: I don't know.

CHAVEZ: You don't know, I don't know what happened [*sic*]? Did you talk to the police?

O. M.: Yes.

CHAVEZ: What happened with the police?

O. M.: We fought.

CHAVEZ: Huh? What happened with the police?

O. M.: The police shot me.

CHAVEZ: Why?

O. M.: Because I was fighting with him.

CHAVEZ: Oh, why were you fighting with the police?

O. M.: I am dying...

CHAVEZ: OK, yes you are dying, but tell me why you are fighting, were you fighting with the police?

.....

O. M.: Doctor, please I want air, I am dying.

CHAVEZ: OK, OK. I want to know if you pointed the gun [to yourself] at the police.

O. M.: Yes.

CHAVEZ: Yes, and you pointed it [to yourself]? [*sic*] at the police pointed the gun? [*sic*] Huh?

O. M.: I am dying, please...

.....

CHAVEZ: OK, listen, listen I want to know what happened, OK?

O. M.: I want them to treat me.

CHAVEZ: OK, they are do it [*sic*], look when you took out the gun from the tape [*sic*] of the police...

O. M.: I am dying...

CHAVEZ: OK, look, what I want to know if you took out [*sic*] the gun of the police?

O. M.: I am not telling you anything until they treat me.

CHAVEZ: Look, tell me what happened, I want to know, look well don't you want the police know [*sic*] what happened with you?

O. M.: Uuuggghhh! my belly hurts...

.....

[16]

CHAVEZ: Nothing, why did you run [*sic*] from the police?

O. M.: I don't want to say anything anymore.

CHAVEZ: No?

O. M.: I want them to treat me, it hurts a lot, please.

CHAVEZ: You don't want to tell [*sic*] what happened with you over there?

O. M.: I don't want to die, I don't want to die.

CHAVEZ: Well if you are going to die tell me what happened, and right now you think you are going to die?

O. M.: No.

CHAVEZ: No, do you think you are going to die?

O. M.: Aren't you going to treat me or what?

CHAVEZ: Look, think you are going to die, [*sic*] that's all I want to know, if you think you are going to die? Right now, do you think you are going to die?

O. M.: My belly hurts, please treat me.

CHAVEZ: Sir?

O. M.: If you treat me I tell you everything, if not, no.

CHAVEZ: Sir, I want to know if you think you are going to die right now?

O. M.: I think so.

CHAVEZ: You think [*sic*] so? OK. Look, the doctors are going to help you with all they can do, OK? That they can do.

O. M.: Get moving, I am dying, can't you see me? Come on.

CHAVEZ: Ah, huh, right now they are giving you medication.

Justice Stevens concluded that it "is evident from the text [that] both parties believed that [Martinez] was about to die," and he characterized the interrogation as "the functional equivalent of an attempt to obtain an involuntary confession from a prisoner by torturous methods." The findings of the trial court would seem to confirm Justice Stevens's characterization. It found that Martinez

[17]

had been "shot in the face, both eyes were injured; he was screaming in pain and coming in and out of consciousness while being repeatedly questioned." Justice Kennedy elaborated on these findings:

> The transcript...and other evidence considered by the District Court demonstrate that the suspect thought his treatment would be delayed, and thus his pain and condition worsened, by refusal to answer questions....
>
> His blinding facial wounds made it impossible for him visually to distinguish the interrogating officer from the attending medical personnel. The officer made no effort to dispel the perception that medical treatment was being withheld until Martinez answered the questions put to him. There was no attempt through *Miranda* warnings or other assurances to advise the suspect that his cooperation should be voluntary. Martinez begged the officer to desist and provide treatment for his wounds, but the questioning persisted despite these pleas and despite Martinez's unequivocal refusal to answer questions.

Justice Stevens concluded: "In this case no reasonable police officer would believe that the law permitted him to prolong or increase pain to obtain a statement. The record supports the ultimate finding that the officer acted with the intent of exploiting Martinez's conditions for purposes of extracting a statement."

All the justices agreed that the answers given by Martinez were "compelled," "coerced," "involuntary," and obtained without the necessary *Miranda* warnings. All agreed therefore that nothing Martinez said in response to this interrogation could be admitted against him in a criminal case and that admission of any such coerced responses would violate his privilege against self-incrimination.

But here the agreement ends and the major dispute begins: namely, what is the extent of Martinez's rights under the Fifth Amendment? Did he have a right "to remain silent"? Did he have a right not to be coerced into making self-incriminating statements? Or was his only right not to have his coerced statements used against him in a criminal case? Put another way, does the Fifth Amendment provide a *primary* right to remain silent or only a *secondary* right to a particular *remedy*—namely, *exclusion* of coerced statements? Is the privilege against self-incrimination only an *exclusionary rule*, or does it also contain an important *substantive right* to remain silent? Or not to be coerced or compelled to admit crimes?

Put yet another way: What is the point of impact of the privilege? At the point when compulsion is employed? Or only at the point when—and if—its fruits are admitted against the coerced person at his criminal trial?

This is not merely a "technical" disagreement. The stakes for all Americans are extremely high, especially in an age of terrorism, when preventive intelligence—information not intended to be used in criminal cases—is often gathered by coercive means, including the threat to withhold medical treatment for extreme pain. As we move closer to the preventive state and further from the deterrent state—as the paradigm begins to shift from after-the-fact punishment to before-the-fact prevention—there will be more emphasis on securing preventive intelligence information as distinguished from self-incriminating confessions to be used in criminal cases.

The Thomas view (shared by five other justices), taken to its logical conclusion, means that the privilege against self-incrimination has nothing to say about the *means* employed by government to extract information from an American citizen (or anyone else), *so long as* the information is not used against the citizen at his criminal trial. In other words, the government may, without violating the privilege against self-incrimination, *torture* a citizen into providing intelligence information deemed necessary to prevent a terrorist attack *or any other feared harm.* There are no apparent limits to this power under the Thomas view of the privilege, except that the fruits of the coercion may not then be admitted in a criminal case against the person coerced. But following the terrorist attacks of September 11, 2001, the Justice Department announced that its "number one priority" was now "prevention," and that prevention was even "more important than prosecution." Since eventual admission of the fruits in a subsequent criminal trial is often not the object of the interrogation—as it was not in the Martinez case—there will be little incentive to the police to forbear from coercion, especially if they are immunized from civil liability.

To be sure, there may be other provisions of the Constitution, particularly the due process clause, that prohibit or limit torture (or other forms of coercive interrogation). That remains to be seen. Some justices and scholars reject the view that due process imposes any *substantive*—as distinguished from *procedural*—constraints on government. The text of the due process clause would seem to support such a limitation: "nor be deprived of life, liberty or property, without due process of law." The *substantive* rights protected by this clause are life, liberty, and property; the *procedure* required to deprive a person of those substantive rights is "due process of law."

Others take the view that the due process clause does impose substantive constraints, but that only the most extreme forms of torture are violative of due process. Justice Thomas, in his opinion, takes a narrow view of due process:

Chavez's questioning did not violate Martinez's due process rights. Even assuming *arguendo*, that the persistent questioning of Martinez somehow deprived him of a liberty interest, we cannot agree with Martinez's characterization of Chavez's behavior as "egregious" or "conscience shocking." ... Moreover, the need to investigate whether there had been police misconduct constituted *a justifiable government interest* given the risk that key evidence would have been lost if Martinez had died without the authorities ever hearing his side of the story. (emphasis added)

Under this standard, coercive interrogation would be constitutionally permissible if its purpose were to serve a "justifiable government interest." Here the government interest was relatively minor: protecting police officers from possible civil liability by getting Martinez to admit he was at fault. (Thomas's statement that the authorities' interest was in "hearing his side of the story" is sophistry. They wanted him to confirm *their* side of the story.) If the governmental interest were far more compelling—the prevention of terrorism, for example—the degree of coercion could presumably exceed even that used here without violating either due process or the privilege against self-incrimination.

The five majority justices on the due process issue did not conclude that the conduct in this case rose to the level of a substantive due process violation. They simply remanded the case to the lower court for a determination of whether Martinez could "pursue a claim" that his right to substantive due process had been violated.

The current law of substantive due process, as it relates to police interrogation, is in a state of disarray. In *Graham v. Conner* (490 U.S. 386 (1985)) the Court ruled that where "a particular amendment provides an explicit textual source of constitutional protection against a particular sort of government behavior, that amendment, not the more generalized notion of substantive due process, must be the guide for analyzing these claims."

What does this ruling mean with regard to the claim made in this case? Martinez argued that the interrogation in his case violated the privilege against self-incrimination, which in his view provides "an explicit textual source of constitutional protection against [the] government behavior." A majority of the Supreme Court disagreed. Does that mean that the case could now be decided under substantive due process? Or must it still be decided— *against* Martinez—under the privilege against self-incrimination, because it is the text of that more specific provision of the Fifth Amendment that "must be the guide for analyzing" his claims? In one sense, the interrogation in *Martinez* is plainly "covered" by the privilege against self-incrimination, as evidenced by the conclusion—agreed to by all nine justices—that its fruits would be inadmissible in any criminal prosecution against Martinez. But the majority ruled that the "coverage" provided by the Fifth Amendment does not require a *remedy* other than exclusion.

It is difficult to predict, therefore, whether the Supreme Court will hold, in a case like Martinez's, that the privilege "covers" the interrogation, and that this provision of the Fifth Amendment rather than "the more generalized notions of substantive due process must be the guide for analyzing these claims."

Even if claims of abusive interrogation can survive the "covered by" a specific amendment test and be considered under "substantive due process," the criteria for establishing a violation of substantive due process are not easy to satisfy. The test for determining whether government action violates substantive due process has long been whether it "shocks the conscience." That test was first articulated by Justice Felix Frankfurter in the 1952 case of *Rochin v. California*, which involved an effort by three

California deputy sheriffs to retrieve capsules, reasonably believed to be unlawful drugs, from the stomach of a suspect who had swallowed them during a police search:

> At the direction of one of the officers a doctor forced an emetic solution through a tube into Rochin's stomach against his will. This "stomach pumping" produced vomiting. In the vomited matter were found two capsules which proved to contain morphine.

The Supreme Court ruled:

> This is conduct that shocks the conscience. Illegally breaking into the privacy of the petitioner, the struggle to open his mouth and remove what was there, the forcible extraction of his stomach's contents—this course of proceeding by agents of government to obtain evidence is bound to offend even hardened sensibilities. They are methods too close to the rack and the screw to permit of constitutional differentiation.

In so ruling, the court analogized the conduct at issue in the *Rochin* case to coercing a confession:

> It would be a stultification of the responsibility which the course of constitutional history has cast upon this Court to hold that in order to convict a man the police cannot extract by force what is in his mind but can extract what is in his stomach.

The "shocks the conscience" test has been controversial from the very beginning. Justice Scalia mocks it mercilessly. In a style typical of the Court's most cynical justice, Scalia accused the majority opinion, in a case that invoked *Rochin*, of resorting to hyperbole and of "resuscitat[ing] the *ne plus ultra*, the Napoleon Brandy, the Mahatma Gandhi, the Cellophane of subjectivity, th' ol' 'shocks-the-conscience' test." He explained his references in a footnote: "For those unfamiliar with classical music, I note that the exemplars of excellence in the text are borrowed from Cole Porter's 'You're the Top,' copyright 1934." He argued, in other words, that the issue of whether police misconduct rises to the level of shocking the conscience is as subjective as whether a particular type of brandy is the best.

It is impossible to predict how the Court will evaluate claims of substantive due process brought by victims of police abuse in preventive interrogation cases or other interrogations in which the fruits of the coercion are not used against the suspect in a subsequent criminal prosecution. In light of this uncertainty—which itself provides a defense against tort suits based on alleged due process violations—the Court's decision that coercion alone does not violate the right not to incriminate oneself will encourage police to employ coercion in situations involving preventive intelligence.

In the chapters to come, I use the *Martinez* case as a window into broader issues relating to the history and policies underlying the privilege against self-incrimination, as well as into the trend toward turning what many citizens have long regarded as broad human rights into narrow criminal trial rights. I also use the *Martinez* case to explore the various modes of constitutional analysis used by the justices and by mainstream scholars in interpreting the Constitution in general and the privilege against self-incrimination in particular. Finally, I use the *Martinez* case as a prism through which to glimpse the future of the privilege in the preventative state toward which we seem to be moving.

CHAPTER THREE

The Limits of Textual Analysis in Constitutional Interpretation

ANY EFFORT TO interpret a constitutional provision must *begin* with its text. The problem is that many provisions are ambiguous, unclear, cryptic, open-ended, and subject to multiple interpretations that may all be reasonable, at least on their face. Human language, particularly legal and political language, cannot begin to capture the complexity and nuance of human thought, action, and interaction. Oliver Wendell Holmes Jr. wisely observed, "A word is not a crystal, transparent and unchanged. It is the skin of a living thought and may vary greatly in color and context according to the circumstances and time in which it is used." Lewis Carroll put it more contentiously:

> "When I use a word," said Humpty Dumpty in a rather scornful tone, "it means just what I choose it to mean—nothing more nor less...."
>
> "That's a great deal to make one word mean," Alice said in a thoughtful tone.

"When I make a word do a lot of work like that," said Humpty Dumpty, "I always pay it extra."

As we shall see, some words that appear in our Constitution are entitled to significant overtime pay plus bonuses, while others require little or no work at all.

According to one school of constitutional interpretation, the words of that document must be interpreted as the framers understood them at the time they became part of the Constitution. But it is not always easy to retrieve the "original understanding" or to adapt it to a legal (or political) system that has changed considerably over the centuries. For example, the prohibition against "cruel and unusual punishments" contained in the Eighth Amendment was written before there were prisons capable of holding convicted defendants for long periods of time. The common punishments of the time included hanging, branding, stockades, warning out, and banishment, but not long-term imprisonment. It is difficult to extrapolate the understanding of the framers to the current practice of sentencing repeat petty offenders to life imprisonment under "three strikes" statutes. Moreover, the Fifth Amendment's prohibition against double jeopardy is limited to "life or limb." Its words do not explicitly cover imprisonment or fines (which were imposed at the time of the framing), despite the fact that subsequent clauses of the same Fifth Amendment talk about deprivations "of life, liberty or property." Literally read, therefore, the double jeopardy clause could be deemed applicable only to the death penalty and physical mutilation, but not to deprivation of liberty or property.

Another instance is the prohibition against "excessive bail." The framers understood that provision as permitting denial of bail—that is, no pretrial release—in capital cases. It is difficult, if not impossible, to determine whether this understanding translates into denial of pretrial release for current defendants charged with crimes that *were* punishable by death at the time of the ratification but that are *now* punishable only by imprisonment. Many crimes that are today not capital were capital at the time of the enactment of the Bill of Rights precisely because there were no prisons and therefore no long prison sentences. (There were short-term jail sentences.)

Once long-term imprisonment became an available alternative, many crimes previously punished by death became punishable by imprisonment. What is uncertain is whether capital crimes were deemed nonbailable because the extreme *punishment* the defendant faced—namely, execution—provided a strong incentive for fleeing, or because of the supposed *dangerousness* of most capital crimes and the fear that the defendant might commit harmful dangerous crimes while awaiting trial. If the former, the historical argument for pretrial release of noncapital defendants today would be strong. If the latter, the case for preventive pretrial detention of dangerous defendants would be compelling. But because nearly all *dangerous* crimes were *also capital* crimes at the time the Bill of Rights was ratified, it is unlikely that the framers ever focused on which of these two possible rationales explained the nonbailability of capital crimes. If that is the case, then there is no original understanding with regard to the current bailability of noncapital, yet dangerous crimes.

It is certainly possible that some of the framers of open-ended provisions—such as "equal protection of the laws," "due process," "cruel and unusual punishment," "excessive bail," and "unreasonable searches and seizures"—deliberately wrote them in a manner that would permit common-law courts to do what common-law courts have always done: to "evolve" differing interpretations over time, place, and circumstance. After all, the framers certainly knew how to write unambiguous provisions that do not permit of varying judicial interpretations. The age requirements for president, senators, and members of Congress are not "maturity," "experience," or "seniority"—words that would require interpretation. They are "thirty five," "thirty," and "twenty five" years of age—words that are self-defining. The requirement for ratifying a treaty is not "a substantial majority," a "supermajority," or a "consensus." It is "two thirds of the Senators present." The amount in controversy that triggers a jury trial in civil cases is not "substantial" or "considerable." It is "twenty dollars"—not even adjusted for inflation!

Into which category, then, do the words of the right against self-incrimination fit? The provision is quite short. "No person ... shall be compelled in any criminal case to be a witness against himself." The Supreme Court, in the 1897 decision *Bram v. United States*, characterized the provision as "concise" and "generic." Some of its words are relatively simple to interpret. The courts have long ruled that "persons" includes not only citizens but also "resident aliens." The framers could, of course, have used the term they used in the Sixth Amendment, "the accused," but they chose the more general word "person." And they placed the privilege not within the Sixth Amendment, which deals only with criminal defendants, but instead in the Fifth Amendment, which deals both with criminal defendants and ordinary people.

"Shall be compelled" is a bit more difficult, because it can bear several interpretations. It could refer only to lawful or formal compulsion, such as that ordered by a judge. Or it could also include extrajudicial and informal compulsion or coercion, such as that employed by police in the interrogation room. (There were no police, at least as we know them today, at the time of the framers, but there was a long history of coercive interrogation.)

"In any criminal case"—words that were added at the last minute without debate—could be defined narrowly to include only criminal *trials* or more broadly to encompass any *investigation* into criminal conduct, or even any proceeding that could *eventuate* in a criminal prosecution.

"To be a witness" could be interpreted to mean only a sworn witness who gives testimony, or it could include unsworn witnesses as well. But giving the word "witness" the former meaning would render the provision meaningless at the time it was written, since defendants were not allowed to testify as sworn witnesses at their own trials.

Interpreted literally and narrowly, the words of the Fifth Amendment do not grant a person the right to remain silent. And that is what Justice Thomas concluded. But that cannot end the inquiry, because the same sort of literal, narrow reading would also permit the introduction of *evidence* obtained *prior to trial* by police or judicial coercion. Indeed, it would allow the government to use the unsworn recorded statements admittedly coerced from Martinez, were he to have been placed on trial for assault with a deadly weapon—a conclusion that appears to have been categorically rejected by the entire court in *Martinez*.

The words of the Fifth Amendment say nothing about *evidence*, though some contemporaneous state constitutional provisions used that word. The Fifth Amendment refers only to "a witness." Read literally, it prohibits the government only from compelling a person to *testify*—that's what "a witness" does— "against himself" in "any criminal case." Its words do not prohibit the *police* from testifying about—or playing a recording of—what the defendant said when he was merely a suspect and not yet a witness, after the police compelled him to speak but before the criminal trial began. Nor does it prohibit a *clerk* from reading the transcript of testimony the person was compelled by a judge to give in a noncriminal case. So long as the defendant himself is not called as an actual witness by the prosecution and compelled to give live testimony against himself at the criminal trial itself, the text of the Constitution—literally read, as Justice Thomas said it should be—is not violated.

Yet Justice Thomas had no doubt that "statements compelled by police interrogations *of course* may not be used against a defendant at trial." But, *of course*, why not? Certainly not because of the text itself, which would seem to authorize the admissibility of such "statements," as long as they were testified to *by the police* and not *the defendant*—so long as the *defendant* was not compelled to be "a witness against himself." Yet Thomas seems to be saying that "the admission *into evidence* in a criminal case of *confessions* obtained through coercive custodial questioning" would violate "the right protected *by the text* of the Self-Incrimination Clause." But plainly it would not, because "the text" of that clause says nothing about *evidence* of confessions secured by the police before trial by coercive questioning. Thomas simply makes up his textual reference. He chides Justice Stevens for his "indifference to the text of the Self-Incrimination Clause." But what Thomas did was worse: he *selectively* cites and then *selectively* shows indifference to the text, as it fits his result. He cites "the text" for a proposition it does not contain: the exclusion of testimony by the police of out-of-court confessions they coerced from the defendant. For the text of the Fifth Amendment to support the exclusion of evidence produced by the prior out-of-court compulsion or coercion of the defendant, it would have to include words such as the following: "and no *evidence* that is the product of compulsion or coercion of the defendant shall be admitted against him at his criminal trial." Several state constitutions at the time of the framing contained language that would support the exclusion of all "evidence" that derived from compelled self-incrimination, but the text of the Fifth Amendment is silent about *evidence* and is limited to prohibiting the government from compelling a person "to be a *witness* against himself."

Justice Thomas cites several cases to support his view that the privilege does require the exclusion of *statements* compelled by police interrogations as well as *testimony* compelled by judges, but that it does not prohibit the compulsion itself. As we shall see, those cases (and others, not cited by Thomas) are inconsistent and inconclusive as to the proper interpretation of the privilege. By citing judicial precedents, however, Justice Thomas seemed to acknowledge that the text alone is not dispositive. According to Justice Thomas and the other justices who joined his opinion, precedent matters as well—at least sometimes. Justices Thomas and Scalia have argued that precedent should be ignored, indeed overruled, when it is inconsistent with the text—at least sometimes.

These justices chose to rely primarily on precedent—at least selectively—rather than literal textual analysis, in concluding that police may not testify about incriminating statements they compelled the defendant to make prior to his trial. But they chose to rely primarily on literal textual analysis in concluding that a person—in this case, Martinez—had no right not to be compelled or coerced to answer self-incriminating questions, so long as his answers were not admitted against him at his criminal trial.

To be sure, there is considerable precedent supporting the view that evidence of pretrial coerced confessions cannot be admitted against a criminal defendant at his trial, despite the absence of specific textual support for that conclusion in the relevant words of the Fifth Amendment. There is no direct precedential support for the conclusion that the privilege against self-incrimination is violated at the point when compulsion is employed, rather than at the point when its fruits are admitted at the criminal trial. But nor is there any direct support for the opposite view. It was an open question prior to *Martinez*.

In deciding to employ a largely textual analysis, the Court disregarded earlier precedents pertaining to the proper *mode of interpreting* the cryptic words of the Fifth Amendment. An 1897 Supreme Court decision expressly considered whether it *only* prohibited the government from calling a defendant *as a witness* at his own criminal trial—the literal meaning of the words used in the Fifth Amendment—or whether it *also* prohibited the government from introducing, through *other witnesses*, evidence of *statements* the defendant was compelled to make prior to trial. The Court rejected the literal interpretation and concluded that "the generic language of the Amendment was but a crystallization of the doctrine as to [out-of-court] confessions, well settled when the Amendment was adopted."

In other words, the constitutional text did not exhaust its intended or understood meaning. Its future applications were left "to be evolved from the facts of each particular case"—a process well known to the common-law framers of the Constitution.

The words of the privilege had to be read against the background of law and practice at the time of the enactment of the Bill of Rights. They could not be wrenched out of their literal context and read abstractly as if they were simply a collection of syllables, as Thomas essentially did. Put another way, these exact same words would mean something very different if they had been written by the framers of the French, German, Russian, or Louisianan constitutions, since those framers would understand these same words to mean something quite different because of their very different legal systems. As Wittgenstein once observed, "If a lion could talk, we could not understand him." If a framer of the Fifth Amendment could talk about how he understood the criminal justice system, and how the words of the Fifth Amendment fit into it, we would have considerable difficulty understanding him, as we shall see later, when we examine the near-contemporaneous opinion of Chief Justice John Marshall in the Aaron Burr case.

A review of the history of the various rights and privileges relating to compelled self-incrimination, as well as of the original understanding of the relevant fifteen words of the Fifth Amendment, will establish that there is no dispositive history nor coherent "theory" or singular understanding that compels any particular reading of the text as it applies to the issue before the court in *Martinez*. There are, on the face of the text, several operative concepts at work.

The first is that the right applies to all persons, not just to those accused of a crime, since the amendment began with the broad words "no person," as distinguished from the words "the accused" which cabin the scope of the Sixth Amendment. This choice of the word "person" seems inconsistent with other words in the same amendment, most particularly "in any criminal case" and "witness against himself." Only an "accused" can, in theory, be a witness against himself in a criminal case (though, in practice, at the time of the ratification, he could not be). The original amendment, as proposed, did not contain the words "in any criminal case." These narrowing words were added at the last minute, and without explanation, by Congressman John Laurence, a Federalist lawyer from New York. The apparent reason for this undebated addition was to deal with a specific problem relating to a legislative conflict between the proposed Fifth Amendment and the bill that would become the Judiciary Act of 1789. Had the right against self-incrimination been a separate amendment in the Bill of Rights, it would have been simple to conform the remaining words to the rest of the amendment by changing "no person" to "no accused," but this change was not made, and so we are left with both broad and narrow language in the same constitutional amendment. Since the right remained in the broader Fifth Amendment rather than having been moved to the narrower Sixth Amendment, both the broad and narrow understandings have plausible textual and

historical claims to being true to the "original understanding."
More realistically, there was probably *no* original understanding as
to whether "no person" or "criminal case" was the intended limiting phrase. The controversies that eventually might turn on re-
solving future interpretive questions, such as the one before the
Court in *Martinez*, probably never occurred to anyone at the time.
No "original understanding" can be ascribed to framers who had
no understanding of the particular problem at issue in a subsequent case.

The second operative concept—and certainly a central one—
is reflected by the words "nor shall be compelled." Compulsion
lies at the core of the prohibition. Freely given statements, even
the most incriminating, were welcome. This may sound obvious, but under the law of other societies, even freely given self-
incriminating statements could not be relied on by the courts.
Under traditional Jewish law, for example, no person could voluntarily incriminate himself. External evidence, usually in the
form of two witnesses, was required. If this seems somewhat
strange to the modern ear, recall that this is essentially the constitutional rule that still governs all treason prosecutions, which
require two witnesses, except that a confession "in open court"
will suffice. But other than for treason prosecutions, and a handful
of exceptional situations, noncompelled statements, whether
made in or out of court, can be admitted into evidence against a
defendant and can form the basis for a conviction.

Compulsion, therefore, is a gravamen of the evil sought to be
prohibited by the Fifth Amendment. But is it compulsion *alone*, or
must the compulsion produce self-incrimination? And if so, must
the self-incrimination be used against the defendant in his
"criminal case"? Does the answer to these questions depend on
whether the means of compulsion employed—judicial torture,
for example—is a sufficient stand-alone evil worthy of indepen-

dent prohibition? As we shall see, at least some of the framers probably thought so, though the issues were never deconstructed so neatly.

The remaining words, "in any criminal case to be a witness against himself," would seem to narrow the prohibition considerably. Even without the words added at the last minute ("in any criminal case") the final words, "a witness against himself," would appear to limit the prohibition only to compelled self-incrimination and not to compelled statements that incriminate others or provide merely preventive intelligence or otherwise useful general information. But recall that these words could not have been intended to be read literally, since no defendant in "any criminal case" *could* be "a witness against himself," even in the absence of the Fifth Amendment.

How, then, should these fifteen words be interpreted? The answer is that they cannot be *interpreted*, as I am using that word and as it is commonly used in, for example, biblical interpretation. Interpretation requires that there be a correct meaning. It is a search for truth: a quest, a discovery. For those who believe that God wrote the Bible and that every word has a true meaning, the job of interpreting becomes crucial. Words used in one part of the Bible are compared with the same or similar words used in other parts of the Bible. No word is considered redundant, or inapt, or erroneous. That is an understandable canon of construction for a divinely authored text. Were the Bill of Rights written by God, interpreters would devote enormous energy to trying to figure out precisely what God meant when He ordained that trial by jury was required in all common law cases involving twenty dollars or more. Why twenty and not ten or fifty? Why not adjust for inflation? We don't engage in that interpretive inquiry—in that effort to discover external truth—when we seek to give meaning to fallible human writings. We are content to conclude that the framers of the Seventh Amendment simply messed up by not adjusting for inflation or absurdly demanding that all common law cases, regardless of how trivial, be tried by jury. And we should be content to conclude that the human framers, limited in their experiences, simply never thought of some of the issues we confront today. Biblical interpreters, who believe they are interpreting the word of God, cannot leave it at that!

Thomas Jefferson, in a revealing and self-deprecatory letter to Samuel Kercheval in 1816, argued for a critical view of the Constitution:

> Some men look at constitutions with sanctimonious reverence, and deem them like the ark of the covenant, too sacred to be touched. They ascribe to the men of the preceding age a wisdom more than human, and suppose what they did to be beyond amendment. I knew that age well; I belonged to it, and labored with it. It deserved well of its country. . . . But I know also, that laws and institutions must go hand in hand with the progress of the human mind. As that becomes more developed, more enlightened, as new discoveries are made, new truths disclosed, and manners and opinions change with the change of circumstances, institutions must advance also, and keep pace with the times. We might as well require a man to wear still the coat which fitted him when a boy, as civilized society to remain ever under the regimen of their barbarous ancestors.

Jefferson was making the case for periodic constitutional change, but a similar case could be made for constitutional *construction* of a flawed human document, rather than for *interpretation* of a sacred covenant.

This is certainly true with regard to the Fifth Amendment. We cannot interpret it, as I am using that word. We must *construe* it. I mean here to distinguish *discovery* from *invention*. Interpretation entails the discovery of an existing reality, such as the Mississippi River or the laws of gravity. Construction entails invention: the building of a sound edifice, code of laws, or work of art. The foundation for invention is discovery, but invention takes discoveries and builds on them.

Some constitutional provisions can be interpreted, in the sense that the singular intention of the framers can be discovered by historical research. It is impossible, however, to interpret the relevant words of the Fifth Amendment, in the sense of discovering the singular understanding behind them, because there was no such understanding. Nor can such an understanding be discerned by parsing the words, since the words appear to conflict with each other. The courts therefore have construed—or, in the words of Marshall, "expounded"—the provision to try to make sense of the garble left by our imperfect framers and to make their imprecise words applicable to changing conditions. The courts have essentially stricken the word "witness" from the text, because it could not have been understood to refer to a criminal defendant called to give sworn testimony at his own trial. Instead of the word "witness," the courts have essentially substituted the following words: "to give an in-court or out-of-court statement that could be testified to by another witness."

Justice Thomas seemed perfectly content with this judicial construction (or excision) because it makes sense of the provision and gives it meaning even in a system in which defendants were precluded from testifying. Justices Stevens, Kennedy, and Ginsburg would construe (or excise) the words "witness against himself" in the context of cases in which "torturous methods" or their "functional equivalent" were used. In such cases, the right would be violated by the extreme compulsion itself without regard to whether its fruits are subsequently used against the defendant in his criminal trial.

Each of their excisions does violence to some of the words of the Constitution in order to give meaning to other of the words. Yet one was acceptable to all of the justices, while the other was rejected by most of them. No textual explanation is offered to justify one excision but not the other. Yet as we shall see, the history and understanding of the provision would not seem definitively to prefer one excision over the other. This is the problem, among others, of selective literal interpretation of texts that cannot rationally mean exactly what they appear to say.

In focusing primarily on the text, the Court not only ignored the history at the time of the founding, as we shall see in more detail in chapter 5; it also disregarded, in the words of Justice Kennedy, "the understanding that has prevailed for generations now," namely, that Americans have a "right to remain silent," or at least "a right not to be compelled to incriminate themselves." This *long-term* understanding, as distinguished from the *original* understanding, deserves some weight, at least according to Justice Kennedy, who wisely cautioned:

> To tell our whole legal system that when conducting a criminal investigation police officials can use severe compulsion or even torture with no present violation of the right against compelled self-incrimination can only diminish a celebrated provision in the Bill of Rights. A Constitution survives over time because the people share a common, historic commitment to certain simple but fundamental principles which preserve their freedom. Today's decision undermines one of those respected principles.

Surely this widespread and long-term understanding of "the right to remain silent" in the face of police or judicial compulsion should be given some weight in interpreting the privilege. It should be given at least a vote, if not a veto. The term "precedent" has both a broad and a narrow meaning. Justice Kennedy was referring to precedent in its broad meaning of "a common historic commitment" to a shared understanding. Justice Thomas invoked the narrower meaning of prior specific cases and doctrines, such as immunity. It is to that narrower view that we now turn.

CHAPTER FOUR

The Limits of Precedent: Which Way Does the "Immunity" Analogy Cut?

IN ADDITION TO ITS UNCONVINCING textual analysis, the Thomas opinion in *Martinez* invoked immunity as an analogy to support its conclusions. On its face, this argument seems like a slam dunk. If a person's "right to remain silent" may be trumped by granting him use immunity—a legislatively authorized and judicially enforced promise that whatever self-incriminating statements he is compelled by the law to make will not be used against him at a subsequent criminal trial—then he never really had an absolute constitutional right to remain silent. All he ever had was a constitutional right not to have compelled testimony *used against him* at his criminal trial.

But this is an argument that goes either too far or not far enough. If there is no constitutional right to remain silent, why does there *need* to be legislation to trump it? Why couldn't a judge—even absent an immunity statute—simply compel any person (other than a criminal defendant at his own criminal trial) to answer self-incriminatory questions? The *consequence* of such compulsion would be the constitutionally required *exclusion* of the answer in his subsequent criminal case, but the person would have no constitutional right, even without a formal grant of immunity, to refuse to answer any otherwise proper question put to him in a civil case, a legislative hearing, or someone else's criminal trial.

But the Supreme Court has been crystal clear—for more than a century—that *absent* a formal grant of immunity, a person has an absolute right to *remain silent* when a judge or other public official seeks to compel him to answer incriminating questions. As the Supreme Court said in 1972: "The privilege ... usually operates to allow a citizen to *remain silent* when asked a question requiring an incriminatory answer." Indeed, the Court has been clear that the scope of the immunity must be at least "coterminous" with the scope of the privilege, or else the person retains the right to remain silent. Simply put, the witness who is given immunity and compelled to answer incriminating questions must end up in the same position—at least as a matter of constitutional theory—as he would have been in had he been allowed to refuse to answer. This long line of cases rests on the assumption—sometimes expressed, more often implied—that absent a grant of immunity, a person has a constitutional right to remain silent in the face of an incriminating question.

The Supreme Court in *Murphy v. Waterfront Commission* acknowledged—in a footnote—that there may be some "conceptual difficulty of pinpointing the alleged violation of the privilege on 'compulsion' or 'use,'" the precise issue that eventually came before the Court in *Martinez* some forty years later. The Court stated, "The constitutional privilege against self-incrimination has *two* primary interrelated facets: The Government may not *use compulsion* to elicit self-incriminating statements; and the Government may not permit the *use in a criminal trial* of self-incriminating statements elicited by compulsion." The Court said, however, that since the states and the federal government are now both constitutionally bound by the privilege, it was not necessary to be "concern[ed]" with deciding the precise point of impact of the privilege: compulsion or use. (In the interests of full disclosure, I must acknowledge that as Justice Goldberg's law clerk in 1964, I drafted that footnote.)

Eight years later, in *Kastigar v. United States*, the Court reaffirmed the right of witnesses to assert the privilege against self-incrimination "in any proceeding, civil or criminal, administrative or judicial, investigatory or adjudicatory; and it protects against any disclosures that the witness reasonably believes could be used in a criminal prosecution [against him] or could lead to other evidence that might be so used." The Court then went on to analyze how immunity statutes impact this right:

> Immunity statutes, which have historical roots deep in Anglo-American jurisprudence, are not incompatible with these values. Rather, they seek a rational accommodation between the imperatives of the privilege and the legitimate demands of government to compel citizens to testify....
>
> The constitutional inquiry, rooted in logic and history, as well as in the decisions of this Court, is whether the immunity granted under this statute is coextensive with the scope of the privilege. If so, petitioners' refusals to answer based on the privilege were unjustified, and the judgments of contempt were proper, for the grant of immunity has removed the dangers against which the privilege protects. If, on the other hand, the immunity granted is not as comprehensive as the protection afforded by the privilege, petitioners were justified in refusing to answer, and the judgments of contempt must be vacated.

The Court then went on to rule that derivative use immunity is coextensive with the scope of the privilege:

> This is a very substantial protection, commensurate with that resulting from invoking the privilege itself. The privilege assures that a citizen is not compelled to incriminate himself by his own testimony. It usually operates *to allow a citizen to remain silent* when asked a question requiring an incriminatory answer. This statute, which operates after a witness has given incriminatory testimony, affords the same protection by assuring that the compelled testimony can in no way lead to the infliction of criminal penalties. (emphasis added)

In other words, a citizen has the right to remain silent unless he has formally been given, either by the legislature or the court, a functionally coextensive right via the mechanism of derivative use immunity. That is the *Kastigar* rule, a rule that has been applied now in a long and uninterrupted line of cases.

Has the Court now overruled, *sub silentio*, this line of cases? Can a judge now compel a witness in a civil case, a legislative committee, or someone else's criminal trial to answer incriminating questions, *even absent a formal grant of immunity*? Why not, if the privilege includes *only* an exclusionary right and not any primary right to remain silent? If there is no independent right not to be compelled or coerced, why can't a judge require a witness to answer *all* questions on pain of contempt?

Justice Stevens, in his opinion in *Martinez*, seemed to worry that the majority had indeed overruled the entire *Kastigar* line of immunity cases that presupposes a constitutional right to remain silent in the absence of coterminous immunity. He observed, "It should come as an unwelcome surprise to judges, attorneys, and the citizenry as a whole that if a legislative committee or a judge in a civil case demands incriminating testimony without offering immunity, and even imposes sanctions for failure to comply, that the witness and counsel cannot insist the right against compelled self-incrimination is applicable then and there."

It is possible, of course, that the Court will eventually rule that although there is no *absolute* right to remain silent, there is some sort of *conditional* right. In other words, absent a formal grant of immunity, every witness has the right to remain silent, but that right disappears when he is given such immunity. But what is a *conditional constitutional right*, and how can a legislative authorization to grant immunity trump a right granted by the Constitution?

One answer is, it doesn't! The person being compelled to answer with a grant of immunity knows that his answer is no longer self-*incriminating*, since it can never be used against him in a subsequent criminal case. Consider the following analogy: A state has a statute making adultery a crime. A witness is asked whether he committed adultery. He refuses to answer based on the constitutional right against self-incrimination. The legislature then enacts a law decriminalizing adultery; the witness can no longer refuse to answer. The legislature has not trumped the witness's constitutional right, it has merely eliminated a condition necessary for its invocation. Or consider a state with a five-year statute of limitations for a given crime. Before the expiration of the statute a witness may refuse to answer questions about that crime, but after it has expired, he must answer. The immunity, the decriminalization, and the expiration of the period of limitation all have one consequence in common: they take the "crim" out of "self-in*crim*ination," thus eliminating an essential element for invoking the privilege. (Of course, statements compelled by a grant of immunity may still be self-incriminating in the sense that they admit to conduct that is criminal, but the Supreme Court long ago ruled—not without dissent—that the right against compelled self-incrimination does not protect against mere infamy, but only against criminal prosecution.)

The situations just referenced—a formal grant of immunity, a legislative act of decriminalization, and a statute of limitations—are very different from the situation confronting Martinez, who had no advanced legislative or judicial guarantee that his answers could not be self-incriminating. So far as Martinez knew—if he "knew" anything, considering the pain and fear he was expressing—he was being compelled to confess to the crimes of resisting arrest and taking a gun from and pointing it at a police officer. Neither the officer nor Martinez understood that the statement he was being coerced into making could not be used against Martinez if he were charged with a crime. Justice Thomas said that this doesn't matter:

> We fail to see how Martinez was any more "compelled in any criminal case to be a witness against himself" than an immunized witness forced to testify on pain of contempt. One difference, perhaps, is that the immunized witness *knows* that his statements will not, and may not, be used against him, whereas Martinez likely did not. But this does not make the statements of the immunized witness any less "compelled." ... Moreover, our cases provide that those subjected to coercive police interrogations have an *automatic* protection from the use of their involuntary statements (or evidence derived from their statements) in any subsequent criminal trial. ... This protection is, in fact, coextensive with the ... immunity mandated by *Kastigar* when the government compels testimony from a reluctant witness. Accordingly, the fact that Martinez did not *know* his statements could not be used against him does not change our view that no violation of the Fifth Amendment's Self-Incrimination Clause occurred here.

There are so many logical, empirical, precedential, and historical errors packed into this one paragraph that it is difficult to know where to begin. First, it begs the question of why immunity is required—if it still is—in the context of judicial compulsion. If a judge were to simply compel a witness to answer incriminating questions, without mentioning immunity, exclusion of that testimony and its fruits would, under the Thomas interpretation of the privilege, be just as "automatic" as would be the exclusion of the fruits of coercive police interrogation. Why, then, is a formal grant of immunity required to engage in the redundant act of assuring subsequent exclusions when such exclusions are constitutionally "automatic" anyway? Or, to ask the question somewhat differently, why is a formal grant of immunity *not* required before the police may compel a suspect to make a self-incriminating statement?

To test Justice Thomas's analogy between formal immunity and police coercion, consider what the situation would be like if a legislature were to enact a statute (or a judge issue an order) explicitly authorizing the sort of compulsion employed against Martinez—according to Justice Stevens, "the functional equivalent of . . . torturous methods"—but providing the sole remedy of exclusion. This would be something like the "ticking bomb torture warrant" proposal I made several years ago, but without the ticking bomb.

No legislature has seriously considered "legitimating" torture by enacting a "torture warrant" or "torture immunity" procedure, even in the ticking bomb situation. The reason legislators are willing to authorize grants of immunity in the context of *judicial* and other *formal* proceedings is because they are prepared to say that *it is right* for a government official to compel answers to otherwise incriminatory questions under a judicial threat of contempt if everyone knows that these answers cannot be used against the

THE LIMITS OF PRECEDENT

person in a criminal case and are thus no longer incriminatory. But the same legislators would be far more reluctant to say that *it is right* to *torture* a person into confessing any crime (especially a routine crime) simply because the confession would be excluded from a subsequent criminal trial. Immunity may well eliminate the gravamen (or at least *a* gravamen) of the self-incrimination violation in the context of an orderly judicial or other formal proceeding, but it would not eliminate it in the context of torture or other forms of extreme coercion. The visual image of a violation of the privilege for most Americans remains the police beating or torturing a confession out of a person in their custody: the old "third degree."

It would seem to follow from the Thomas analogy that once a person is given immunity, he can be compelled *by any means* to provide incriminating evidence. Yet the only means available by law is the threat of contempt, fine, and imprisonment. If these means fail—as they did, for example, in the well-known case of Susan McDougal—could the state then resort to physical compulsion, even torture? If Justice Thomas's analysis of the privilege is taken to its logical conclusion, the answer would be yes—at least under the privilege. Yet no one would seriously consider authorizing torture following a grant of immunity and the failure of imprisonment to compel the testimony in routine cases.

Justice Thomas's narrow reading of the text of the privilege seems to support the conclusion that immunity is not constitutionally required before a witness can be compelled to answer self-incriminating questions. The text limits the privilege to "any criminal case." In a civil case or a legislative hearing, there is no textual prohibition against compelling testimony. And since compelled or coerced testimony, according to Thomas, will be "automatically" excluded from "any criminal case" in which the person is a defendant, it would seem to follow that a formal grant

[47]

of immunity should no longer be required as a prerequisite for imprisoning a witness who refuses to answer self-incriminating questions.

Justice Thomas's analogy between the kind of coercive interrogation employed in *Martinez* and a legislative grant of immunity is deeply flawed. There is a critical difference between the lawful act of a legislature in explicitly authorizing immunity and the unlawful and unauthorized act of a rogue policeman beating up a citizen, even if that unlawful act may have a *consequence* similar to that resulting from the lawful grant of immunity. To assume, as Justice Thomas does, that the difference has *no* constitutional significance is to beg the crucial question.

Justice Thomas is also wrong in confidently asserting that the protection in the case of a police beating is "automatic." Any experienced criminal lawyer knows that exclusion is anything but "automatic" in such cases. The fact that immunity has been given to a witness cannot be disputed by the prosecution. It is part of a court record. It shifts a heavy burden of proof to the prosecution to show an independent source for all of its evidence. A claim of police coercion, on the other hand, faces difficult, sometimes insurmountable obstacles. Coercion is a matter of degree. Immunity, on the other hand, has either been bestowed or it hasn't. You can't be a "little bit immunized." But you can be a little coerced, and in close cases no one can know for certain whether a court will find coercion or not. Moreover, the alleged coercion will often occur in a setting where the only witnesses, other than the accused, are police officers who have a motive to minimize or deny the use of coercive methods. Having the defendant testify at a coercion hearing is often risky. Judges often err on the side of believing the police. As Chief Justice Warren Burger wrote (when he was on the Court of Appeals): "It would be a dismal reflection on society to say that when the guardians of its security are called to testify in court under oath, their testimony must be viewed with suspicion." An experienced trial judge, Irving Younger, disagreed: "With all possible deference, I disagree. When there are grounds for believing that 'the guardians of its security' sometimes give deliberately false testimony, it is no 'dismal reflection on society' for Judges to acknowledge what all can see." Even when the police interrogation is recorded, which it rarely is in instances of real coercion and physical abuse, there will be difficult issues of line drawing and interpretation.

The trial dynamics in a case involving a formal grant of immunity and one involving a claim of coercion are very different, as any experienced criminal lawyer would know. Yet Justice Thomas rejects this reality and accepts instead the highly questionable conclusion—previously rejected by the Court—that a defendant who has been coerced into making self-incriminating statements is in at least as favorable a position as a defendant who has been compelled into making such statements by a formal grant of immunity. Indeed, Justice Thomas overrules this critical aspect of *Kastigar* without even mentioning it. He cites *Kastigar* in *support* of his conclusion that there is no difference between a formal grant of immunity and the supposedly automatic immunity that follows from police coercion, when *Kastigar* explicitly says the opposite. Here is what Kastigar says:

> [A] defendant against whom incriminating evidence has been obtained through a grant of immunity may be in a stronger position at trial than a defendant who asserts a Fifth Amendment coerced-confession claim. One raising a claim under this statute need only show that he testified under a grant of immunity in order to shift to the government the heavy burden of proving that all of the evidence it proposes to use was derived from legitimate independent sources. On the other hand, a

defendant raising a coerced-confession claim under the Fifth Amendment must first prevail in a voluntariness hearing before his confession and evidence derived from it become inadmissible.

Even if the exclusion of coerced testimony were automatic—which it is not—it does not follow that a *prediction* of *future* judicial exclusion is the constitutional equivalent of legislatively authorized formal immunity. The Supreme Court addressed this precise issue in *Pillsbury Co. v. Conboy* and ruled that a witness retained his right to remain silent even though it was virtually certain that his answers—derived directly from testimony he had given under a prior grant of immunity—would be excluded from his criminal trial as the derivative fruits of his earlier immunity:

> Unless the grant of immunity assures a witness that his incriminating testimony will not be used against him in a subsequent criminal prosecution, the witness has not received the certain protection of his Fifth Amendment privilege that he has been forced to exchange.... The District Court below essentially predicted that a court in any future criminal prosecution of Conboy will be obligated to protect against evidentiary use of the deposition testimony petitioners seek. We do not think such a predictive judgment is enough.

The Court reiterated its *Pillsbury* holding in the 1998 case of *United States v. Balsys*. Yet Justice Thomas in *Martinez* ignored *Pillsbury*, citing only a concurring opinion in that case, while overruling it *sub silentio*.

The analogy between legislatively authorized formal immunity and "automatic" exclusion that supposedly follows from unlawful police coercion is not only incomplete, it is fundamentally flawed.

At best, the precedent of immunity cuts both ways in the context of *Martinez*. The immunity case law, especially *Kastigar*, *Pillsbury*, and *Balsys*, cuts strongly against it. It is certainly not the slam dunk Thomas makes it appear.

Indeed, taking Thomas's decision to its logical conclusion, one could plausibly argue that the immunity precedent supports the argument that the point of impact of the privilege is when the coercion occurs. The syllogism would go something like this:

A) No person may constitutionally be compelled to incriminate himself unless he is first given immunity coterminous with his privilege.

B) If the point of impact of privilege were not at the point of compulsion, then any witness could be compelled to provide incriminating testimony.

C) It follows therefore, that the point of impact—or at least *a* point of impact of the privilege—is when compulsion is employed.

It all depends on the premise you begin with.

Justice Thomas's misuse of the immunity precedent illustrates the limitations of analogy as a tool of constitutional interpretation. As an old Yiddish expression cautions: "'For instance' isn't an argument." Life unfolds on a continuum, but law must construct lines and categories that are often artificial, at least at the edges. This reality makes it dangerous to put too much stock in analogies that may be artificial.

As with his textual argument, Justice Thomas's immunity argument goes either too far or not far enough. Taken to its logical conclusion, its reasoning overrules more than one hundred years of precedent requiring an explicit grant of immunity before a witness can be compelled to answer self-incriminating questions.

That goes too far. If its reasoning does not overrule the immunity cases, then it is difficult to understand why the police should be empowered to coerce a suspect into making self-incriminating statements without a prior formal grant of immunity. Moreover, since exclusion is not the sole remedy for a violation of the witness's privilege in the absence of immunity—he retains his right to remain silent—why should it be the sole remedy for a violation of the suspect's right not to be coerced into surrendering his right to remain silent? The majority opinions in *Martinez* failed to address these issues in their rush to deny coerced individuals the right to sue for a violation of their constitutional right.

A more persuasive analogy—although also an imperfect one—would be to the use of coercion against a witness to elicit incriminating statements against *another* person. The court has not placed any limitation on the interrogation methods used against suspect A to incriminate suspect B, but this may be because B has no standing to complain about methods used against A if these methods produce "other"-incrimination, as distinguished from "self"-incrimination. It does not follow, however, from B's lack of standing to complain about the methods used against A, that A lacks standing to seek injunctive relief or damages, even if he is not the individual against whom the incriminating statements will be used. A may well have standing to complain about coercive methods used against him, regardless of whether the statements coerced from him are self- or other-incriminating. The question is whether his complaint is properly grounded in the right against self-incrimination or in the due process clause. It begs that question to assume that the right against self-incrimination has no bearing on this issue. It all depends on whether the word "compelled" is more or less central to the right than the word "himself." The answer to this textual question may lie, at least in part, in the history of the right itself.

To summarize: A plain reading of the fifteen words of the right against compelled self-incrimination would lead to the following limitations:

1) It would apply only when a criminal defendant is a compelled *witness* at his own trial—a limitation that would have rendered it largely irrelevant at the time it was ratified and that has been rejected.

2) It would not apply to *evidence* testified to by others (such as policemen) of coerced self-incriminating statements made before the criminal case began—a limitation that has also been rejected.

3) It would apply only at the point when the prosecution seeks to *introduce* the compelled self-incriminating statement at the defendant's criminal trial, and not at the point when *compulsion is employed* to elicit the statement. This would leave a witness with no right to refuse to answer incriminating statements and no right to be given formal immunity before he is compelled to answer—a limitation that has also been rejected by the Court.

4) It would not limit the type or degree of coercion that can be applied to a person in an effort to elicit incriminating statements, so long as the coerced statements (and their fruits) are not introduced against him at a criminal trial—a limitation that was accepted by a majority of the Supreme Court in *Chavez v. Martinez*.

The question, therefore, is why the Supreme Court has *rejected* the first three plain-meaning limitations on the text of the right against compelled self-incrimination, and then felt it necessary to *accept* the fourth limitation. Does the answer lie in the history or original understanding of the right? It is to that issue we now turn.

CHAPTER FIVE

. . .

The Limits of Historical Inquiry

MANY OF THE FOUNDATIONAL CASES interpreting the privilege against self-incrimination purport to rely on history. As Justice Felix Frankfurter once observed: "The privilege against self-incrimination is a specific provision of which it is peculiarly true that 'a page of history is worth a volume of logic.' " History cannot, however, always be found on "pages," or even websites. It is often more complex, multifaceted, and inaccessible than judicial opinions or legal briefs make it appear. Advocates' history, or as Leonard Levy has called it, "law office history," often consists of the artful selection of "historical facts from one side only, ignoring contrary data, in order to support, rationalize, or give the appearance of respectability to judgments resting on other grounds."

Remarkably, the majority opinion in the *Martinez* case never mentions history. Nor does it seek to unearth the provision's original understanding, though Justice Thomas is often the first to cite history when it supports his views. This selective resort to history raises important questions regarding the appropriate use of history in constitutional interpretation that I shall address in the coming pages.

Any honest attempt to reconstruct the history underlying the privilege against self-incrimination will necessarily be incomplete, impressionistic, and probabilistic. This will be especially so when the sources consulted are primarily judicial and secondary. The object of such an inquiry can rarely be the discovery of a singular truth. Historians seek coherent stories, but history itself generally unfolds in a more disorderly way. As Søren Kierkegaard said, "Life can only be understood backward, but must be lived forward." But life understood so differently from how it is actually lived often produces distortions by those who seek to recount it. The privilege against self-incrimination developed over a period of time when record keeping was spotty, practice often differed from theory, necessity sometimes trumped articulated norms, and law enforcement was relatively primitive.

The early history of what came to be the modern right against self-incrimination also developed against the background of European political, religious, and ideological conflicts, some of which were less familiar to the New World.

Justice Robert Jackson aptly described the quest to recapture history in the context of discerning the understanding of the framers: "Just what our forefathers did envision, or would have envisioned had they foreseen modern conditions, must be divined from materials almost as enigmatic as the dreams Joseph was called upon to interpret for Pharaoh."

The object of any historical inquiry must therefore be modest: to convey a sense of how the relevant issues were understood, considered, addressed, and rationalized during the period of time in which the privilege developed and the constitutional provision was drafted. Identifying historical errors, especially the common error of judging history through the prism of modernity, is a less difficult task. Reconstructing the prisms through which the framers and their contemporaries actually viewed the problems associated with the privilege is more daunting.

Moreover, the way the question is posed can affect the outcome of the inquiry. For example, the question can be put quite specifically in an effort to respond to the precise question before the court in *Martinez*: At the time of the framing, was there an independent right, under the privilege against self-incrimination, not to be compelled by government officials to provide self-incriminating information? Or was the right merely a remedy that prohibited the government from using compelled information against the individual at a criminal trial?

That question might be difficult to answer, because the framers never posed it in this dichotomous fashion. Indeed, I have come across no explicit recognition of the dichotomy that was central to the issue posed in *Martinez* until it was raised by Justice Arthur Goldberg in a footnote to his 1964 opinion in *Murphy v. Waterfront Commission* and left unresolved. Several legal historians with whom I conferred acknowledged as well that they had seen no explicit reference to this dichotomy before or at the time of the ratification. There are, however, several subquestions that may help answer the primary question:

- Could a person who was being subjected to coercion bring an injunctive legal action to prevent or stop the coercion, or was his only remedy exclusion at a subsequent criminal trial?
- Could he bring a lawsuit for damages resulting from coercive interrogation, even if the compelled statement was never used against him at a criminal trial?
- Were judges or other officials ever disciplined for improperly compelling an individual to testify, even if no com-

pelled statement was used against the individual at a criminal trial?

- Was the remedy of exclusion mandated for all violations of the privilege, or only for some? If only for some, what remedies, if any, were available for others?

- Did the law explicitly authorize the use of coercion or compulsion under any circumstances? If so, which?

- Were certain methods of interrogation absolutely prohibited, regardless of the use to which the information would eventually be put? If so, how was the prohibition enforced?

- Were there any explicit discussions, in the scholarly or judicial literature, of the difference between the *application* of coercion and the *evidentiary use* of the resulting information?

- Were there any explicit references at common law to the gathering of *preventive intelligence* information, as contrasted with information to be used to *incriminate* the coerced suspect at his own trial?

- Was there any articulation of a right to remain silent at common law, and if so, were witnesses ever warned or advised of this right?

- Were there any analogies to immunity? If so, was compulsion authorized in cases in which a witness had the functional equivalent of modern immunity? Was any kind of compulsion, such as torture, forbidden even in such cases?

- In situations where it was unclear whether a witness would eventually become a criminal defendant, was he accorded a privilege not to respond to potentially incriminating questions?

- If a witness in a state proceeding claimed fear of being prosecuted by a sister state, by the federal government, or by another nation, could he refuse to answer incriminating questions?

- Were the relevant words of the Fifth Amendment understood by the framers to prohibit certain methods of interrogation? Or were they intended only to provide a remedy of exclusion if these methods were employed? If the former, was there any understanding about remedies available to enforce such a prohibition?
- Were there circumstances under which an individual could refuse to incriminate others? Or refuse to provide general or preventive information?

Subquestions of this kind designed to help reconstruct the framing generation's understanding of the privilege fall into several categories. The first asks what the contemporaneous institutions—especially the courts—actually *did*, rather than *said*. If there were *remedies*—in addition to or instead of exclusion—for alleged violations of a right to remain silent or a right not to be coerced or compelled into making self-incriminating statements, that would be evidence of an independent right. If there were no such remedies, that fact alone would not conclusively negate the existence of such a right because there were many rights in those days without well-developed remedies. But the absence of any remedy would weaken the claim that there was an independent right.

The framers clearly intended to constitutionalize certain *existing* common law rights and privileges as they understood them. But not all the framers and certainly not all the ratifiers were lawyers. Some had a technical, legal understanding of existing rights, and others had a broader, more philosophical or political understanding of such rights. If a legislative body were today to seek to codify "the right to remain silent" or "the presumption of innocence" or the prohibition against "cruel and unusual punishments," there would be different contemporaneous understandings of these rights.

Moreover, in every era, there will be differences between what is preached and what is practiced. For example, Jeremy Waldron, in arguing recently that it is "dispiriting as well as shameful to have to turn our attention to [the] issue of torture" in the post-9/11 world, quotes with approval an article in the 1911 edition of the *Encyclopedia Britannica* that asserts that the "whole subject [of torture] is now of only historical interest as far as Europe is concerned." That absurd position could be maintained only if one looked exclusively at what Europeans were *saying* about torture and not at what they were *doing*. Torture by Europeans was extensively practiced by the French in North Africa, by the British in India and Kenya, and by the Belgians in the Congo. It was used extensively during the First and Second World Wars. It is probably fair to characterize the twentieth century as the "torture century" and Europe as its "capital." But one would not recognize this reality by reading proclamations, statutes, judicial decisions, encyclopedias, or law review articles.

R. H. Helmholz is more perceptive than Waldron when he observes that "legal history is filled with instances where in hindsight practice in the courts does not seem to measure up to the ideals professed by thoughtful men and women of the time." And if one adds to "practice in the courts" practice in the streets, back alleys, detention centers, lockups, and military theaters, the disparity becomes even greater.

It is for this reason, among others, that posing focused questions about what the courts were doing in fact—a variant on Holmes's famous definition of law as "the prophecies of what the courts will do in fact"—is an important window into the contemporaneous understanding of the right that was constitutionalized by the fifteen words of the Fifth Amendment dealing with self-incrimination.

If the historical answers to the subquestions were to point uniformly and definitively in one direction (as, for example, the history of trial by jury in criminal cases points uniformly to twelve men, unanimous juries), and if there were a high level of confidence in the accuracy of the material as well as in the absence of other material that points in a different direction, then it might be possible to conclude that history answers the specific question posed in this case: Did the framing generation understand there to be a right not to be coerced, or only a right to exclude the fruits of compulsion? But if the answers to the subquestions point in differing directions, or if there is no convincing evidence that the framers ever considered the question, or if there is evidence that the framers (or some of them) understood the right as broader than how the courts applied it, then the historical material might be helpful but not definitive. That state of affairs—which is probably more usual than not—is rife with potential for abusing history by picking and choosing only those elements that suggest a particular outcome, while ignoring elements that may undercut it. Judicial opinions are filled with examples of such selective misuses of historical material. The "ransacking" of history, as one expert has put it, is a game played by ideologues of every stripe. As Maitland quipped more than a century ago, the "seamless web" of history is torn by telling only a piece of it. The web is torn even more when the piece to be told is selectively wrenched out of context by an ideologue with a contemporary agenda.

Another common method of misusing history is to cite it only when it supports one's ideology and to ignore it when it undercuts one's ideology. This selective recourse to history has characterized the opinions of many justices over time, including the author of the *Martinez* case and some of his colleagues who joined his opinion. This is part of a larger problem of judicial interpretation: every method of interpretation is selectively invoked or ignored as it serves the interests of ideological result orientation.

In this analysis of the scope of the privilege I rely on the primary research of others who are more expert than I am at accessing, translating, and contextualizing the original sources. My own expertise lies in my combined experience as a criminal lawyer and teacher and my ability to see practical connections that may be more difficult for historians to find in the preserved written record, which is necessarily incomplete, especially as to the dynamics of typical, as distinguished from high-profile, cases. It may also lie in my experientially induced skepticism that the preserved records always mirror the practices they purport to report. With history, as with criminal law, the absence of evidence is not necessarily evidence of absence. These caveats should be borne in mind as we turn to the history.

THE EARLIEST HISTORY OF THE RIGHT
AGAINST SELF-INCRIMINATION

Elements of what eventually became the right against self-incrimination appear in early religious jurisprudence even before the emergence of the Anglo-American system of criminal justice. In the 1653 trial of John Lilburne—to which, according to Dean Erwin Griswold, "we owe the privilege of today"—reliance was placed on the laws of God and the rules prevailing in ancient Israel. Lilburne argued that for the state to compel him to answer incriminating questions "would be contrary to the laws of God, for that law requires no man to accuse himself." Lilburne seems to indicate that such was the practice of the courts in Palestine, "for Christ himself in all his examinations before the high priest would not accuse himself but upon their demands returned back, Why ask you me? Go to them that heard me." In the *Miranda* decision,

Chief Justice Earl Warren, in asserting that the "roots" of the privilege "go back into ancient times," specifically cited Jewish law, as enunciated by Maimonides: "The principle that no man is to be declared guilty on his own admission is a divine decree."

The traditional Jewish approach to self-incrimination is, however, significantly different from the Anglo-American approach. Under Jewish law, confessions are never admissible against a criminal defendant, even if they are voluntary. The prohibition is not against *compulsion*; it is against *self-incrimination*. The principle is "A man cannot represent himself as wicked" ("Ein adam messim atsmo rasha"). This principle grows out of the legal system established by the Bible, which demands two external witnesses and disqualifies the defendant himself (as the common law rule did) from testifying.

It is also possible that the Jewish prohibition against voluntary self-condemnation may reflect the religious prohibition against suicide. Maimonides, a twelfth-century doctor and codifier, wrote of those who confess as perhaps being among "those who are in misery, bitter in soul, who long for death, thrust their sword into their bellies or cast themselves down from roofs." The rule against self-incrimination may have been designed, in part, to preclude the legal system from becoming a vehicle for judicial suicide. (At common law as well, "to furnish testimonial evidence against himself with or without oath, was likened to drawing one's blood, running oneself upon the pikes, or cutting one's own throat with one's tongue.")

The current American legal system, in contrast, welcomes—even rewards—confessions of guilt, as long as they are voluntary. A criminal defendant has a constitutional right to testify on his own behalf. He also has the right to admit guilt in order to garner anticipated sentencing benefits from his cooperative attitude and/or actions.

Analogies to other legal systems, therefore, are relevant but imperfect. There are, however, some insights that can be gained by looking at common concerns. Several relevant cases are recounted in the Talmud, as described by Simcha Mandelbaum:

> [A] person was charged with setting fire to a neighbor's property on Sabbath. Judgment was requested for money damages as well as penalties for the violation of the rules of the Sabbath. The defendant offered his own confession in evidence. It was decided that the testimony should be admitted only as it related to the civil suit and not for the purpose of criminal conviction. A similar solution was offered by the Jewish court in another case where a woman was seeking the court's permission to remarry. She contended that her former husband, who had disappeared from home, was dead. To establish the husband's death, she called a witness who testified that he himself killed the husband. The court granted the requested permission to the woman. The court in its opinion stated that although the testimony was self-incriminatory in nature, the court could split the testimony and accept the part which established the death of the husband. The court added that such testimony could not be used to convict the witness for murder.

These cases suggest an early, commonsense variation on what eventually became "immunity." The witnesses were permitted to make self-incriminatory statements for use in civil cases, but the statements were excluded in the criminal cases. Even here, however, the analogy to the modern privilege is incomplete, because the witnesses in these cases were not *compelled* to make self-incriminating statements; they volunteered to do so. Under Jewish law the gravamen of the violation was not *compulsion*; it was *self-incrimination* in the context of criminal cases. Since the confession was not being used in the criminal case, there was no violation of the self-incrimination principle and the gravamen never occurred. It would beg the question to assume that in the context of the modern privilege, compulsion is not at least part of the gravamen of the violation.

Many legal systems developed pragmatic ways to circumvent or limit constraints on prosecuting the guilty. In Jewish law, for example, if there was only one reliable witness and no advance warning, the murderer would not simply be let free, perhaps to kill again. Rather, an informal mechanism of incapacitation was developed by the rabbis to mitigate the rigors of the biblical requirements.

The same must have been true for the privilege. When societies desperately needed information—for example, when the king's life was believed to be in danger—they got it, regardless of what the law permitted or forbade. Sometimes, the law provided explicitly for exceptional situations, as with the "torture warrant" in sixteenth- and seventeenth-century England and the 1641 statutory directive in Massachusetts to employ torture to elicit the names of "confederates" from convicted capital offenders, as long as the torture was not "barbarous and inhumane." Blackstone justified the use of torture to elicit preventive intelligence as an act of "state" rather than "law." Mostly, though, the law was simply ignored or circumvented. The way of the hypocrite—proclaiming virtue while practicing vice—has been a constant throughout history.

THE LEVY HYPOTHESIS

Professor Leonard W. Levy, whose book, *Origins of the Fifth Amendment*, won the Pulitzer Prize in history, traces the American right against self-incrimination back to the struggle for religious and political freedom by English dissidents. In his view, the right grew out of reaction to the wrongs associated with the prosecution of such dissidents, most particularly with the oath *ex officio*, which was an important tool of the inquisitorial system. It required dissidents to swear to tell the truth *before* they were charged with a crime, and it empowered their inquisitors to plumb the depths of their most secret thoughts. In other words, after they were compelled to take this open-ended oath, they could be asked, in effect, to confess all of their secret crimes, sins, and disloyal or heretical thoughts, as if to a priest—except that these "priests" could administer earthly punishments, including death.

Levy dates the origin of the English privilege as far back as the thirteenth century, when the oath *ex officio*, or inquisitorial oath, was given as "a gift of Pope Gregory IX":

> The new oath procedure was first used in 1246 when Bishop Robert Grosseteste conducted "strict Inquisitions" into the sexual misconduct and general immorality of the people in his diocese. . . . To discover all who were guilty of any of the seven deadly sins, the noble and humble alike were put to the *oath de veritate dicenda*, "an innovation never used in the Realm before," and were questioned about themselves and others "to the enormous defamation and scandal of many."

The oath *ex officio* continued to be used over the centuries not only by ecclesiastical courts, but by secular tribunals, such as the Star Chamber. It proved to be a powerful, if controversial, weapon against religious and political dissidents. One important shield against this weapon was principled silence, as manifested by an old maxim of the cannon law, *Nemo tenetur seipsum prodere*. Levy translates this as "No man is bound to accuse himself."

[65]

Levy, like Dean Erwin Griswold, points to "Freeborn" John Lilburne, a seventeenth-century Puritan "leveler," as "the most remarkable person connected with the history of the origins of the right against self-incrimination" and credits his "sensational trial" with being "the immediate reason for the abolition of the oath *ex officio.*"

King Henry III "issued writs of prohibition against Bishop Grosseteste in 1246 and 1252 commanding that laymen not be examined under oath in ecclesiastical courts except in matrimonial and testamentary causes." (These writs suggest that exclusion was not the sole remedy for violation of the right in its early history.)

Although Levy, unlike some others, does not trace the right against self-incrimination back to the Magna Carta in 1215, which granted rights only to nobles in relation to their king, he credits the *spirit* of the Great Charter with providing a stimulus for the invocation of the right as part of the guarantee that no man shall be condemned except by the law of the land. The Court of Star Chamber—as the king's council came to be called because it met in a room "whose ceiling was ornamented with stars"—employed an oath similar to the one that was so central to the ecclesiastic courts. These oaths, in essence, required those who came before these courts to incriminate themselves by acknowledging their guilt under oath. The widespread opposition to this inquisitional process was, at least in part, responsible for a fundamental reinterpretation of the Magna Carta. Levy pointed to numerous dissidents who invoked the Magna Carta in support of their right against self-incrimination: "Because the canon law was against them, suspects had to be creative and invented the claim that conscience and the Magna Carta authorized a right against self-incrimination.... [This] fiction... in time reached the stature of an article of constitutional faith that the Magna Carta outlawed forcing a person to be a witness against himself."

The origins of the right against self-incrimination, according to Levy, cannot thus be fully comprehended without considering its religious and political background:

The claim to the right emerged in inquisitorial examinations, initially conducted by the Church, then by the State. It emerged also in the context of the great political struggle for constitutional limitations on arbitrary prerogative; during the late sixteenth century and early seventeenth, it was a focal point in that struggle to establish individual liberties and more representative government.... The claim to this right also emerged in the context of a whole cluster of criminal procedures whose object was to ensure fair play to the criminally accused. It harmonized with the principles that the accused was innocent until proved guilty and that the burden of proof was on the prosecution. It was related to the idea that a man's home should not be promiscuously broken into and rifled for evidence of his reading and writing. *It was intimately connected to the belief that torture or any cruelty in forcing a man to expose his guilt was unfair and illegal.* It was indirectly associated with the right to counsel and to have witnesses on behalf of the defendant, so that his lips could be sealed against the government's questions or accusations.... Above all, the right was most closely linked to freedom of religion and speech. (emphasis added)

In light of this rendition of history, it is not surprising that Levy concludes that the right against self-incrimination was well established by the time the Bill of Rights was ratified at the close of the eighteenth century. He quotes a 1735 pamphlet by Benjamin Franklin that supported a minister's right to refuse to submit his dissident sermons to a commission of inquiry, arguing that such compulsion "is contrary to the common rights of mankind, no man being obliged to furnish matter of accusation against himself." He also cites several cases from colonial New York, Pennsylvania, Massachusetts, and other colonies to the effect that "the right against self-incrimination was ... firmly fixed." By 1776, "several states elevated the common-law right against self-incrimination to the status of a constitutional right." Thus, when the privilege was ratified in the Fifth Amendment in 1793, it was uncontroversial. According to Levy, it was, at the very least, "a ban on torture and a security for the criminally accused," but "these were not the whole of its functions":

> The framers understood that without fair and regularized procedures to protect the criminally accused, there could be no liberty. They knew that from time immemorial, the tyrant's first step was to use the criminal law to crush his opposition.... The Fifth Amendment was part and parcel of the procedures that were so crucial, in the minds of the framers, to the survival of the most treasured rights.... Above all, the Fifth Amendment reflected their judgment that in a free society, based on respect for the individual, the determination of guilt or innocence by just procedures, in which the accused made no unwilling contribution to his conviction, was more important than punishing the guilty.

This broad view of the political and religious history of the right against self-incrimination and of its established status by 1793 has been vigorously disputed by some legal historians, prominent among them Professor John Langbein of Yale Law School.

THE LANGBEIN HYPOTHESIS

John H. Langbein, whose groundbreaking research has revolutionized our understanding of the development of the adversary system of criminal justice, argues that the origins of the contemporary privilege against self-incrimination lie not so much in the dissent battles over the oath *ex officio* as in the increasing role of defense counsel *following* the ratification of the Bill of Rights. He sees the privilege, therefore, much more in the narrow context of the criminal justice system than in the broader context of political and religious freedom.

His primary argument is that prior to the eighteenth century, there could be no effective privilege because the defendant was, as a practical matter, required to speak (though "not testify") for himself at trial. This was so because an attorney could not speak for him. Unless the defendant personally "respond[ed] to the charges against him," he would effectively be presumed guilty and convicted, because he also "lacked the protection of the modern judicial instruction on the standard of proof." Thus, as Langbein picturesquely summarizes the situation: "The right to remain silent when no one else can speak for you is simply the right to slit your throat, and it is hardly a mystery that defendants did not hasten to avail themselves of such a privilege."

Langbein researched the "pamphlet reports of trials from the 1670s through the mid-1730s," and then "into the 1780s," and found no case in "which an accused refused to speak on asserted grounds of privilege, or in which he makes the least allusion to a privilege against self-incrimination." He concluded therefore that criminal defendants could not, as a practical matter, assert any privilege against self-incrimination. "In a word, they sang."

This all changed, according to Langbein, as criminal defense lawyers became more actively involved in the defense of persons accused of a crime. The system was transformed from the "accused speaks" model—which had little room for a privilege—to the "testing the prosecution" model, in which lawyers did the talking and eventually "suppressed the defendant's testimonial role." It was under this latter model that the modern privilege against self-incrimination developed in practice.

Langbein acknowledges that the theoretical basis for a privilege antedates the emergence of defense counsel and the modern adversary system and has roots deep in Christian as well as Jewish law. A Christian was obliged to confess his sins to God (or his priestly surrogate) but not to admit his crimes to secular authorities. But Langbein's "key insight" is that

> the maxim did not make the privilege. It was rather the privilege—which developed much later—that absorbed and perpetuated the maxim. The ancestry of the privilege has been mistakenly projected backwards on the maxim, whereas the privilege against self-incrimination in common law criminal procedure was, in truth, the achievement of defense counsel in the late eighteenth and early nineteenth centuries.

Langbein insists that the privilege

> became functional only as a consequence of the revolutionary reconstruction of the criminal trial worked by the advent of defense counsel and adversary criminal procedure.

SHIPS PASSING IN THE NIGHT

There are several missing pieces in Langbein's innovative analysis. He deals with only one aspect of the privilege: the right of an already-charged criminal defendant to refuse to speak. The "defendant's privilege" is an important trial right, but it is only part of what ultimately became the triad of rights against compelled self-incrimination.

In reality there are three aspects to the right: the first is the one on which Langbein focuses, the *criminal defendant's privilege*. As understood today, it precludes the government from calling the defendant as a witness at his criminal trial. The defendant does not even have to invoke this right. It is a limitation on the government. If a prosecutor were to say, in front of a jury, "I now call my next witness, the defendant," the right would be violated and a mistrial would almost certainly be declared. Closely related to this limitation on the government is the right of the criminal defendant to decide whether or not to testify on his own behalf, and if he decides not to testify, to have no adverse influence drawn from the exercise of this right. Related to this is the right of a defendant to a jury instruction squarely placing the burden of proof on the prosecution, because if the burden were to be on the defendant, that would undercut his right not to testify. Finally, there is the right to counsel, also under the Sixth Amendment, because, as Langbein astutely notes, in the absence of that important right, there would be no one other than the defendant himself to present the defense case.

The defendant's privilege is not limited to *self-incrimination* or being a witness *against himself*. It is an absolute right *not to be called* or required to testify *at all*, even if his testimony would be self-*exonerating* or *favorable*. A criminal defendant need not assert, suggest, or even believe that his testimony could be self-incriminating as a condition to exercising his right not to testify. He can simply decide, as a tactical matter, that it is in his best interest not to testify.

Langbein is surely right that a self-interested defendant would be unlikely to decline to speak *at all* if his voice was the only one that could be heard in his defense. But to waive one's right to *silence* may not always be the same as waiving one's right against *self-incrimination*. A defendant could, at least in theory, speak *exculpatorily*—that is, assert his innocence and tell an exculpatory story, such as an alibi. Experienced criminal lawyers know, of course, that what sounds exculpatory to a lay client will often sound inculpatory—that is, self-incriminating—to a judge or jury. This would be especially true if the defendant, after telling his exculpatory story, could be questioned—cross-examined—about it by the judge or prosecutor. Langbein, in a conversation with me, said that he was not certain how much, if any, questioning of the unsworn accused took place during the "accused speaks" era, but it is logical to assume that some questioning must have been allowed and that the truthful answers to at least some of the questions would be self-incriminating. It would be interesting for a trained historian to examine the original sources to see whether any defendants who chose to speak on their own behalf told an exculpatory story, then tried to assert the privilege in response to incriminating questions, and if so, whether judges allowed selective invocation of silence after the accused had spoken. That historian's research task is beyond the scope of this book.

Levy does not fully address this issue in his book, but in a subsequent law review article, responding to Langbein and other critics, he makes a related point:

> The fact that defendants spoke does not mean that defendants were forced to confess guilt at their trials. Defendants spoke to deny the charges against them and to repudiate the prosecution's evidence. They invoked the right only when necessary to respond to a question the answer to which might incriminate. . . . Langbein cannot distinguish between a defendant's answering a question by denying the charges and a

defendant's refusal to answer on grounds of self-incrimination. Langbein says that defendants claimed the right in isolated remarks, while "utterly disregarding any supposed privilege against self-incrimination." Supposed? Is Langbein implying that the "privilege" was just a fiction? Indeed, Langbein's point misleads, for the defendant spoke to answer charges, invoking his right only when an answer might incriminate him.

Moreover, Langbein seems to neglect one of the earliest manifestations of the privilege that is central to Levy's hypothesis: the right of a person not to *reveal* crimes of which the authorities *had no knowledge*. One of the great evils of the oath *ex officio* was that it required the person to take "an oath to tell the truth before knowing the charges and accusers." Religious and political dissenters (and in an age when religion and politics were barely distinguishable, dissenters tended to be *both*) were summoned before ecclesiastical tribunals and required to take this oath. If they took it, they, as believing Christians, would be religiously and morally obliged to tell the truth: "In the seventeenth century men did not take oaths lightly." Once the person was under oath, the tribunal would probe him about his opinions, ideas, beliefs, heresies, and loyalties. In that way, they would "ensnare" dissidents into becoming self-confessed criminals.

An early version of the privilege was that "no man had to reveal an unknown crime, but if strongly suspected he was obliged to answer truthfully under oath." The latter part of this formulation (akin more to the Fourth than the Fifth Amendment) soon disappeared, but the earlier part has, of course, remained an essential part of the constitutional right.

Langbein seems to downplay the reality that this aspect of the privilege—not to be compelled to reveal an unknown crime—could operate to the advantage of a suspected dissident even without his having access to counsel. The "accused speaks" system operated only *after* the accused was, in fact *accused*—of a specific crime. At that point, absent counsel, he had every incentive to speak, and whatever privilege he may have had in theory did him little good in practice. But a dissident who was merely suspected— without external proof—of holding heretical or treasonous views had an incentive to remain silent, and many did, even without advice of counsel. To turn a phrase on Langbein: in the context of the oath *ex officio*, the right to remain silent was the right not "to slit your own throat." Thus Levy and Langbein both appear to be correct as to some aspects of the privilege and incorrect, or at least incomplete, as to others.

This right not to reveal unknown or merely suspected crimes became important during the McCarthy era, when people suspected of communist affiliations were compelled to take loyalty oaths or to testify about their beliefs and affiliations. It has also been important in the context of police roundups of suspected criminals, which still occur from time to time. It is certainly among the root sources of the current privilege and dates this aspect of it well before the late eighteenth century, when defense lawyers began to play a more active role in the trials of defendants who could pay them.

In some respects, Levy and Langbein are ships passing in the night. Each is dealing primarily with different aspects of the privilege and different historical sources of what eventually became the multifaceted constitutional right against self-incrimination. Levy, the historian, focuses on the larger political and religious roots of the privilege and on its "symbolic importance." Langbein, the lawyer (and legal scholar), emphasizes its practical applications and its role as part of the adversarial process in action.

The second aspect of the privilege against self-incrimination, the *witness's* privilege, was not the focus of either Levy's or Langbein's hypothesis, but it has played a central role in the American history of the privilege. The witness's privilege does not provide an absolute right to remain silent. If a witness in a case in which he is not the criminal defendant—say, a civil case, a legislative hearing, or someone else's criminal case—is subpoenaed, he *must* take the stand. He cannot refuse to answer questions that might incriminate *others* or that would merely *embarrass* him. To invoke the *witness's* privilege, as distinguished from the *criminal defendant's privilege*, he must have a good faith basis for believing that the answer to a specific question or line of questions might *incriminate* him. He has no blanket privilege *not to testify*, as the criminal defendant does, but only a privilege not to be compelled to *incriminate himself*. The witness's privilege can be neutralized by a formal grant of derivative use immunity, which assures the witness that his self-incriminating answers and their fruits may not be used against him in any subsequent criminal trial. The defendant's privilege cannot be neutralized or trumped by any legal procedure.

The witness's privilege has assumed a political role, since it is often invoked in legislative hearings such as those conducted during the McCarthy era. But it also plays an important role in the legal system, because witnesses frequently invoke it in civil cases and when subpoenaed by the prosecution and/or defense in the criminal trials of others.

The third aspect of the privilege, which grows out of the oath *ex officio* as described by Levy, is the *suspect's* privilege, sometimes called "the confession rule." It focuses on a manner of compulsion entirely different from the defendant's and witness's privileges. In this situation, the suspect is being interrogated by the police, who generally have no subpoena or legal authority to require him to answer *any* questions. He can simply refuse, not because of any constitutional privilege *he* has, but because of the lack of *power* the *police* generally have to compel him to answer. The power of the police derives not from the authority of the subpoena or judicial compulsion, but from the psychological advantage they have in such encounters (as in the *Martinez* case). The courts, therefore, have articulated a suspect's right to regulate the use of police compulsion, usually called "coercion." This right arises in the context of in-custody interrogation, rather than at formal legal proceedings.

These three facets of the privilege, which have now coalesced into the modern Fifth Amendment right against self-incrimination, originated from three distinct, but overlapping, common law rules with somewhat different histories and policies. Langbein is correct that it was not until sometime after the ratification of the Fifth Amendment, when defense lawyers began to play a more active role in criminal trials and the police emerged as an important investigative institution, that the modern privilege became recognizable in its current manifestations. But Levy is also correct in dating the roots of the privilege much further back in time. Moreover, as the wrongs changed, the rights changed as well. The early history of the privilege was intermeshed with political and religious persecutions in which men's thoughts and ideas were on trial. These wrongs, with some striking exceptions, were not carried to the New World. The right against self-incrimination in the New World became more of a legal than a political right, invoked more often by common criminals than by heroic dissidents, except in periods of political persecution, such as that experienced during the McCarthy era.

DISCERNING THE UNDERSTANDING
OF THE FRAMERS

The complex history of the right against self-incrimination makes it difficult to discern the understanding of the framers and apply it to today's very different system of criminal justice. It may be possible, however, to shed some historical light on some of the narrower questions set out earlier in this chapter. Early historical evidence suggests, for example, that the privilege was not merely a remedy of exclusion, but also a right that was enforceable directly against those who employed improper compulsion. Professor R. H. Helmholz reports a fourteenth-century case in which "disciplinary action was initiated against the archdeacon of Ely for having violated the prohibition [by] habitually interrogat[ing] men and women under oath in circumstances where their 'pretended excesses were wholly secret.'" He also reported a similar case in the early fifteenth century.

But Professor Charles M. Gray has pointed out that these cases involving writs of prohibition most often involved interjurisdictional disputes between religious and secular courts, and the writs were designed to preserve the prerogatives of the secular courts. In other words, they were at least as much about power as they were about rights. Still, they suggest that there was more to the privilege and its antecedents than a mere exclusionary right. The focus was not only on subsequent *use* of the evidence but also on the *means* used to compel the self-incriminating statements. This was certainly the case when it came to torture, which was seen as a stand-alone evil. It was probably also true of interrogation under oath, which was seen by some as analogous to torture.

The American historical evidence is consistent with the British. There was a close association between the principles underlying the privilege, as it came to be incorporated into the Fifth Amendment, and the fear of torture and other impermissible methods of interrogation. As Professor Albert Alschuler has reported, "In legislative and convention proceedings, in letters, newspapers, and tracts, in judicial opinions and law books, the whole period from 1776 to 1791 ... a ban on torture and a security for the criminally accused were [seen as] the most important of [the privilege's] functions, as had been the case historically."

In *State v. Hobbs* (1803), the Supreme Court of Vermont seemed to conclude that the state constitution's self-incrimination clause prohibited the use of torture as a means of extracting evidence, regardless of whether its fruits were subsequently admitted into a judicial proceeding. The court held: "All compulsory process to enforce an acknowledgment of guilt is for ever excluded, *not only from our judicial proceedings*, but *all attempts* of individuals to extort confessions by bodily suffering is reprobated" (emphasis added). The court ruled that torture to extract evidence was itself a violation of the common law for which the torturer could be punished. *The point of impact of the violation was when the torture was employed against the suspect, not when its fruits were admitted against him.* The court explained its view of the history of the privilege: "However the practice of torture to extort confession had prevailed in various governments, it certainly never was sanctioned by the common or statute law of our English ancestors for although the rack was occasionally resorted to in the reign of Henry VI and even in the reign of Queen Elizabeth, yet Judge Blackstone observes, *it was used as an engine of state, not of law.*"

The *Hobbs* case presents a close analogue to *Martinez*. The common law understanding of the privilege, which was arguably constitutionalized in the Bill of Rights, was sufficient to punish the interrogator for torture. The court found that the use of torture to extract confessions was "against law, the constitution, and the peace and dignity of the state of Vermont." It is unclear whether the person tortured in that case was ever prosecuted, whether he confessed, or whether any confession was excluded, but it is clear that Vermont's self-incrimination provision was violated by "all attempts of individuals to extort confession by bodily suffering."

Though the court said that an important part of the privilege's justification was the unreliability of a torturously extracted confession, the privilege was cast as a primary right to be free from such coercion, not exclusively as a trial right. Its point of impact was the moment of coercion. It would have been interesting to see what a court would have done if torture had produced self-proving evidence—say, an admission of a fact that only the criminal could know. If there were no concern about "its uncertainty as a criterion of truth," would the torturer have been commended for the truth he elicited, or still condemned for the means he employed to produce that truth? Such are the vagaries of history that we can only speculate on the answer to this unasked question.

Professor Levy may well be correct when he observes that "where there is a right against self-incrimination there is necessarily a right against torture," but the courts and commentators have often been less than clear about whether the "right against torture" stands alone and gives rise to an independent cause of action, regardless of any subsequent evidentiary use.

The right not to be tortured was certainly on the mind of American revolutionaries at the time the Bill of Rights was being considered. Torture was not a distant danger associated by the colonist only with the old regimes of Europe. To the contrary, torture had, in fact, been authorized, in special cases, by Article 45 of the 1641 Massachusetts Body of Liberties:

No man shall be forced by Torture to confess any Crime against himself nor any other unless it be in some Capital case where he is first fully convicted by clear and sufficient evidence to be guilty, After which if the cause be of that nature, That it is very apparent there be other conspirators, or confederates with him, Then he may be tortured, yet not with such Tortures as be Barborous and inhumane.

Note that the primary prohibition includes the use of torture to obtain an incriminating statement against a person "other" than the person being tortured. This suggests that the right may be broader than *self*-incrimination, extending to a right not to be tortured to obtain evidence against anyone. But then the statute takes back that right in the special circumstances described in the exception.

By 1793, a strong consensus had been developed against any use of torture and other impermissible means of securing evidence. Professor Alschuler summarizes the situation as follows: "When the privilege was embodied in the United States Constitution, its goal was simply to prohibit improper methods of interrogation." Even if that was not its only goal—and there is some dispute about this—it seems clear that it was at least one important goal: "Americans of the founding generation unmistakably saw the privilege as a safeguard against torture."

Indeed, Thomas Jefferson would have replaced George Mason's words on compelled self-incrimination with a prohibition against the use of "judicial torture." For these framers, the issue was not only whether coerced statements could be *used* in a criminal trial, but also whether the *process of coercion*—and especially torture—should be prohibited by the U.S. Constitution.

Still, it might be argued that although the *purpose* of the privilege was to prohibit torture and other improper methods of interrogation, the *means* selected by the framers was an exclusionary rule. There is, however, no convincing contemporaneous historical evidence to support the conclusion that exclusion was the *only* means contemplated by the framers. Indeed, there is some evidence that not all governmental conduct that was thought to be prohibited by the privilege had an exclusionary rule as its remedy. And it is unlikely that the framers understood the self-incrimination provision as *authorizing* the use of torture for obtaining *preventive information*, as the sixteenth-century British torture warrant procedure and the seventeenth-century Massachusetts procedure had done. One prominent treatise described the common law as prohibiting all torture, even that directed against a nondefendant: "By the common law of England ... no such engine of power as the rack, or nay other instrument of torture, can be used to furnish the crown with evidence, extorted out of the prisoner's mouth against himself *or any other person.*" This certainly suggests that an exclusionary rule—which would provide no remedy for a nondefendant—was not understood to be the only means of enforcing a right not to be tortured.

Nor is there any persuasive evidence that the framers understood the due process clause of the Fifth Amendment to be the appropriate vehicle for safeguarding against torture. If there was any provision of the Bill of Rights that was understood to prohibit torture it was the privilege against self-incrimination.

It would be much easier for historians, lawyers, and judges today if the framers of the Fifth Amendment had explicitly considered and resolved the precise question, whether the application of torture to a suspect was a stand-alone, independent violation of his constitutional right against self-incrimination, or whether the introduction into evidence of the fruits of such torture was required to complete the violation. But history does not always ask the precise questions to which the current generation seeks answers. We must be satisfied with the historical material that is accessible and reliable, and we must acknowledge that the available sources often provide incomplete answers, as a consideration of two early, important American cases demonstrates.

THE MARBURY AND BURR PRECEDENT

Among the most interesting sources on the original understanding of the privilege are the judicial opinions of Chief Justice John Marshall, one of the nation's greatest jurists, who lived during the founding era and presided over the Supreme Court in the years following the ratification of the Bill of Rights. It so happens that he opined on aspects of the privilege in two of the most important cases in American history.

The first was *Marbury v. Madison*, the decision that established the power of the Supreme Court to review the unconstitutional actions of the executive. In that case, decided just ten years after the ratification of the Bill of Rights, one of the issues was whether the acting secretary of state, Levi Lincoln, could be compelled to answer a question as to "what had been done with the commission" at issue in the case. According to Leonard Levy, he "probably had burned it." The secretary refused to answer on the ground, among others, that he should not be "compelled to answer anything which might tend to criminate himself." Chief Justice Marshall agreed and ruled that Lincoln "was not obliged to disclose anything that might incriminate him." Clearly, then, Marshall understood the right to extend beyond criminal defendants at their own trials and to apply to witnesses in civil cases.

This application of the privilege clearly preceded the development of the adversarial system and the right to counsel as we know them. It could be asserted for the benefit of the witness, without the assistance of counsel.

The second case arose out of the treason trial of Aaron Burr, which has been called "the greatest criminal trial in American history." Marshall's opinion in the Burr case centered on the witness's privilege, but it also touched on the defendant's privilege. The prosecutor asked the accused's clerk whether he "underst[ood]" a ciphered paper. The clerk refused, "saying that the answer might criminate himself."

Marshall upheld the clerk's claim, citing the "settled maxim of law," namely, that "no man is bound to criminate himself." This maxim, he continued, "forms one exception to the general rule ...

that every person is compellable to bear testimony in a court of justice." It is interesting to note that Marshall *did not* cite the Constitution in support of this maxim. This might give rise to the inference that the witness's privilege—as distinguished from the defendant's privilege—was not originally understood to be included within the words of the Fifth Amendment. But Marshall then went on to discuss an aspect of the defendant's privilege, which is undoubtedly covered by the words of the Fifth Amendment, also without referencing the Constitution. Perhaps this was because he understood the Fifth Amendment simply as constitutionalizing the common law and believed that the Constitution should be invoked only as a last resort, if the ordinary law conflicted with it. The grand jury sought to obtain from the defendant Burr himself the ciphered letter. The grand jury "are perfectly aware," according to its foreman, "that they have no right to demand any *evidence* from the prisoner under prosecution [i.e., the defendant] which may tend to criminate himself" (emphasis added). Marshall confirmed the grand jury's view of the law: "The grand jury were perfectly right in the opinion, that no man can be forced to furnish *evidence* against himself" (emphasis added).

This broad view—that a defendant need not produce physical evidence, even documents, that might incriminate him—is not the law today, though it was the law through much of our history.

Another issue was whether the grand jury could "examine" the defendant on issues that were not self-incriminating. The chief justice "presumed that the grand jury wished also to know whether the person under prosecution could be examined on other questions not criminating himself." The answer will be surprising to the modern ear: "The Chief Justice knew not that there was any objection to the grand jury calling before them and examining any man as a witness who laid under an indictment." It is not clear whether the proposed examination would be under oath or unsworn, but it does seem clear that Marshall believed that a criminal defendant who was not yet indicted could be examined, like any other witness, by the grand jury that was considering his indictment, but that, also like any other witness, he could refuse to answer those questions that might be incriminating.

We cannot be certain about any of this, because the issue was mooted by Burr's representation to the court that "the letter is not at this time in my possession."

Another perplexing aspect of Marshall's view of the privilege is his apparent limitation of its application to serious felonies such as treason. He opined that "if the letter should relate to misdemeanor and not to the treason, the court is not apprized that a knowledge and concealment of the misdemeanor would expose the witness to any prosecution whatsoever." It is not clear whether Marshall meant that fear of incrimination for a misdemeanor is never covered by the privilege—an unlikely reading since there were serious misdemeanors at the time that subjected defendants to harsh punishment. The more likely reading is that a prosecution *of this particular witness* on misdemeanor charges was remote, perhaps because it would not be a crime to "conceal" a misdemeanor. This latter reading would support a narrower interpretation of the privilege, and one that would authorize immunity as a technique for trumping the witness privilege.

Another episode that occurred during the Burr trial—President Jefferson's remarkable interrogation of Dr. Eric Bollman—could also lend some support to immunity:

Bollman's confession had been given after the President had voluntarily assured him that nothing he said would be used as evidence to incriminate him. Though Madison had taken notes, Jefferson requested Bollman to put his remarks in writing. The President's letter offered "*his word of honour* that they shall never be used against himself [Bollman], and *that the paper shall never go out of his hand.*" Bollman promptly furnished the President with a signed statement of almost twenty pages.... When the case for an indictment against the arch-conspirator was prepared, the President sent Bollman's signed statement to the United States attorney, George Hay.... Noting that Bollman's statement had been made with the assurance that it "should never be used *against himself,*" Jefferson informed Hay that it would be useful "that you may know how to examine him, and draw everything from him." If Bollman lied on the stand, Hay "should go as far as to ask him whether he did not say so and so to Mr. Madison and myself." To induce Bollman to testify, Jefferson enclosed a pardon. If Bollman refused to appear as a witness, he was to be taken immediately into custody.

These opinions by America's greatest chief justice and these actions by one of America's greatest presidents in America's greatest criminal trial should give pause to anyone seeking to discern *the* original understanding of the Fifth Amendment. Few contemporary American judges would recognize the current privilege against self-incrimination in the rulings of Chief Justice Marshall. Even so central a figure in our own constitutional jurisprudence as Marshall resembles Wittgenstein's lion when it comes to understanding the late eighteenth- and early nineteenth-century privilege against self-incrimination. Its broad outlines are discernable in the maxim "No man is bound to criminate himself," but the details and applications of the modern privilege are difficult to identify.

CAN WE RELIABLY DRAW ANY
HISTORICAL CONCLUSIONS?

Legal history rarely speaks with a clear voice. This is especially so with regard to the history of rights. Rights are often rooted in a recognition of wrongs and a desire to avoid their recurrence. It should follow that the development of rights will be as sporadic, episodic, and inconsistent as the acknowledgment of wrongs. The history of the privilege confirms this thesis.

Consider, for example, the issue of whether the privilege protects a person from revealing information that is shameful, but not criminal. In *Ullmann v. U.S* (1956), the Supreme Court ruled, in an opinion by Justice Felix Frankfurter, "The Fifth Amendment operates only where a witness is asked to incriminate himself—in other words, to give testimony which may possibly expose him to a criminal charge." Justices William O. Douglas and Hugo Black argued in dissent:

> The Fifth Amendment was designed to protect the accused against infamy, as well as against prosecution. . . . The history of infamy as a punishment was notorious. Luther had inveighed against excommunication. The Massachusetts Body of Liberties of 1641 had provided in Article 60: "No church censure shall degrad or depose any man from any Civill dignitie, office, or Authoritie he shall have in the Commonwealth." Loss of office, loss of dignity, loss of face were feudal forms of punishment. Infamy was historically considered to be punishment as effective as fine and imprisonment.
>
> [This] attitude toward infamy was a part of the background of the Fifth Amendment. . . . It was in this tradition that Lord Chief Justice Treby ruled in 1696 that ". . . no man is bound to answer any questions that will subject him to a penalty, or to

infamy." ... When public opinion casts a person into the outer darkness, as happens today [1956] when a person is exposed as a Communist, the government brings infamy on the head of the witness when it compels disclosure. That is precisely what the Fifth Amendment prohibits.

Accordingly, Justices Douglas and Black concluded that immunity from criminal prosecution is not sufficient to protect a witness from the broader evils against which the Fifth Amendment was designed to protect.

Leonard Levy argued that Douglas and Black were essentially correct. He cites numerous instances of dissidents and others refusing to admit conduct that might be shameful but not criminal. But Levy also concluded that history was on the side of those who argued that "a full grant of immunity superseded the witness' right to refuse to answer on grounds of self-incrimination."

These two conclusions seem irreconcilable. If the privilege protects against self-revelation of shameful but noncriminal acts, then immunity cannot trump the privilege, since immunity does not protect against shame. Under a grant of immunity, the person must admit to his shameful behavior; he simply can't be criminally prosecuted for it.

These two conclusions are irreconcilable as a matter of *logic*, but they may both be correct as a matter of *history*. History does not unfold logically. This was especially so in systems, such as the American colonial, that lacked hierarchal judicial review in which a single supreme court authoritatively interpreted a written constitution. There will often be historical events—some even contemporaneous with the other—that speak with different voices or at least with different tones. Advocates seize on the material that supports their view while ignoring material that undercuts it.

Good historians present all the conflicting data and rarely expect a singular conclusion.

Current research on the history of the privilege against compelled self-incrimination suggests that in 1791 it was a work in progress. The multifaceted right, as we know it today, had not yet developed fully, either in theory or in practice. The relevant words of the Fifth Amendment purported to constitutionalize the common law—to take a snapshot of a streaming video. They reflected several *principles* that were deeply rooted in religion and history but were inchoate in *practice*. The criminal justice systems then in existence in the colonies were so different from our current approach that direct analogies are inevitably misleading. During the colonial period, the limited role of counsel in most criminal cases, the pressure on defendants to speak in their own defense, the prohibition on defendants testifying as sworn witnesses, the absence of instructions on not drawing adverse inferences from silence and on the presumption of innocence, the absence of police as we know them today and of backroom interrogations, and other procedural differences relegated the privilege to a largely symbolic role in many cases. Those symbols, however, were apparently of considerable importance to the framers, who were well aware of the abuses still prevalent in parts of Europe and only recently ended in England.

In the years following the adoption of the Fifth Amendment, the role of the privilege changed considerably. It came to be understood as incorporating several different principles, all of which grew out of the history that gradually gave rise to the modern privilege, but none of which was completely developed in 1793. In light of this complex background, it is difficult to find specific historical answers to many contemporary questions, but a few conclusions seem plausible, if not entirely certain:

1. The framers did not explicitly consider the precise question posed by *Martinez*, namely, whether the privilege includes an independent right not to be subjected to coercion, or whether the privilege is limited to the remedy of exclusion. In other words, there was no original understanding regarding the precise issue in *Martinez*.

2. The framers probably understood the privilege as a prohibition on "judicial torture." It is uncertain, however, what understanding, if any, the framers might have had about the remedy or remedies for violating this prohibition, but there is no evidence that they understood exclusion as the sole remedy for torture.

3. The framers probably understood the privilege as prohibiting compelled judicial oaths in at least some contexts. Again, there is little historical evidence of the framers' understanding with regard to remedies. There is some historical evidence that exclusion was not the sole remedy against compelled judicial oaths.

4. Some aspects of the early privilege, most particularly the "suspect's privilege," carried with it an exclusionary remedy. The "witness's privilege" probably did not.

5. There is some evidence that courts sometimes enjoined the coercion of witnesses and may have allowed actions for damages by those who were coerced, or even criminal prosecutions against the coercers. But these tended to be unusual cases that often grew out of interjurisdictional disputes, and so not much can be derived from them in terms of general principles or practices.

6. There are early hints of a sort of functional "immunity" as a tool for compelling self-incriminating statements from

witnesses, though the doctrine was not formally enacted until later.

In summary, there is considerable uncertainty about the original understanding, or understandings, of the privilege against compelled self-incrimination. Was it understood to convey a right to remain silent? And if so, what was the precise nature and scope of that right? Was it understood to apply only to criminal defendants at their own criminal trials? And if so, how can that understanding be reconciled with the practice at this time of not permitting defendants to testify under oath at their own trials? Did it apply to witnesses in legal proceedings other than criminal trials if these witnesses could be subject to later criminal prosecution based on their testimony? (Marshall answered yes.) If so, could this aspect of the privilege be trumped by some sort of immunity? Did the privilege apply to suspects who were being informally interrogated—not under oath—by officials who were more like the police of a later generation (e.g. constable, sheriff) than they were like judges? If so, were there any limits on the nature of the interrogations that could be conducted? Did it apply to certain types of compulsion directed at securing statements from one witness about the crimes of another witness? (Some colonial statutes and cases seem to say yes.) The one historical issue about which there appears to be little disagreement among experts is that the privilege, whatever else it entailed, was understood to include, in the words of Professor Albert Alschuler, "an unqualified prohibition of torture."

A fair reading of the historical material does not support the conclusion that the only remedy understood by the framers to be available to enforce the prohibitions against torture was an exclusionary rule limited to a criminal defendant. Nor does it support the conclusion that the only nonexclusionary remedy for torture

THE LIMITS OF HISTORICAL INQUIRY

would be under the due process clause. It seems likely, though not certain, that the framers understood torture as an evil *separate from* and in *addition to* the use to which incriminating statements could be put at a defendant's subsequent criminal trial. They probably viewed torture as an evil even if it was employed to gather evidence or information for use *other* than in a criminal trial against the individual who was subjected to torture. There is certainly no compelling historical evidence to support the conclusion that the framers understood the Fifth Amendment privilege to authorize— or, to put it more negatively, to not prohibit—the use of torture against persons who would not become defendants in criminal trials. At the time of the ratification of the Fifth Amendment, there was some historical precedent for the use of torture against already convicted defendants to obtain information against their confederates, as well as to secure preventive intelligence against traitors and others who posed security threats. There were also those, most prominent among them the philosopher Jeremy Bentham in Great Britain, who were publicly advocating the return of torture for convicted killers who refused to reveal the whereabouts of their dangerous confederates. There is nothing in the historical record to suggest that the framers intended to incorporate these controversial precedents and proposals as exceptions to the general prohibition against torture.

The historical record on the issue of torture is clearer than on the issues of mere compulsion and coercion. There is no dispositive historical evidence to support the conclusion that coercion short of torture (or compulsion short of the judicial oath) was seen by the framers as an independent evil separate from the evil of using the fruits of such coercion or compulsion against the defendant at his criminal trial. It cannot be said fairly, however, that the historical record supports the opposite conclusion. Nor is there much historical guidance on how to draw the line between torture and extreme coercion, as the Massachusetts legislature tried to do in 1641 when it authorized the use of torture as long as it was not "barbarous and inhumane" (and as the Bush Administration has tried to do more recently).

To summarize the evidence up to now, the text of the right against compelled self-incrimination has been subject to various constructions, excisions, and expansions that do not necessarily compel the conclusion reached by the Court in *Martinez*. Nor does the analogy to immunity compel this conclusion. Neither does the original understanding as reflected by the history at the time of the ratification. Let us turn now to the long-term understanding of the right from the ratification to the present to see whether a clear direction is provided by that developing understanding over time.

CHAPTER SIX

. . .

The Privilege over Time

THE SYMBOLIC ASPECT OF THE PRIVILEGE

In addition to the *original* understanding of the right against self-incrimination—which is ambiguous on several critical issues—it may be relevant to look at the understanding *over time*, and most particularly over recent generations. The Supreme Court often considers such evolving understandings, especially when important aspects of our legal system have grown around them. In fact, the "understanding" of the right against self-incrimination has varied considerably with the times, especially with the abuses experienced in a particular era. It has also varied with the level of abstraction at which the right is described.

At one level, there is the privilege as "symbol," and at another there is the privilege as "law in action." Put another way, there is what lawyers and judges *say* about the privilege, and what lawyers and judges *do* about it in concrete cases. To illustrate this difference, I have prepared a chart contrasting some of the most authoritative and influential statements made about the privilege throughout our history with the holdings of the courts in actual cases.

THE PRIVILEGE AS SYMBOL	THE PRIVILEGE IN ACTION

An Indispensable "Landmark" of a Proud Tradition

"The Fifth Amendment has been very nearly a lone sure rock in a time of storm.... It has, thus, through all its vicissitudes, been a *symbol* of the ultimate moral sense of the community, upholding the best in us, when otherwise there was a good deal of wavering under the pressures of the times." (Erwin Griswold, 1955)

"[A] hallmark of American justice in the last... thirty years."

(Justice Stephen Breyer, oral argument in *Dickerson v. United States* (2000), found in *The Nine* by Jeffrey Toobin at 124)

"Few would be so narrow or provincial as to maintain that a fair and enlightened system of justice would be impossible without... the immunity from compulsory self-incrimination.... Justice... would not perish if the accused were subject to a duty to respond to orderly inquiry." (*Palko v. Connecticut,* 1937)

Bulwark of the Individual versus the Collective

"[The privilege against self-incrimination] is a part of the historical establishment of a balance... between the power of the state and the rights of the individual, which... more than anything else is the

"Under our criminal procedure the accused has every advantage.... Our dangers do not lie in too little tenderness to the accused. Our procedure has always been haunted by the ghost of the innocent man convicted.

THE PRIVILEGE AS SYMBOL	THE PRIVILEGE IN ACTION
essence of modern democracy." (Telford Taylor, 1955)	It is an unreal dream. What we need to fear is the...watery sentiment that obstructs, delays, and defeats the prosecution of crime." (*United States v. Garsson*, 1923)
"The Fifth Amendment was one device in the distribution of power which was designed to tip the scale in favor of the individual against the weight of the state." (Erwin N. Griswold, 1960)	"Despite its cherished position, the Fifth Amendment addresses only a relatively narrow scope of inquiries." (*Garner v. United States*, 1976)

A Protector of Privacy

"[The privilege] reflects many of our fundamental values and most noble aspirations:...our respect for the inviolability of the human personality and of the right of each individual 'to a private enclave where he may lead a private life.'" (*Murphy v. Waterfront Commission*, 1964)	"We cannot cut the Fifth Amendment completely loose from the moorings of its language, and make it serve as a general protector of privacy.... The Fifth Amendment protects against 'compelled self-incrimination, not [the disclosure of] private information.'" (*Fisher v. United States*, 1976)

THE PRIVILEGE AS SYMBOL	THE PRIVILEGE IN ACTION
"Various guarantees create zones of privacy.... The Fifth Amendment in its Self-Incrimination Clause enables the citizen to create a zone of privacy which government may not force him to surrender to his detriment.... The Fourth and Fifth Amendments were described in *Boyd v. United States* as protection against all governmental invasions 'of the sanctity of a man's home and the privacies of life.' " (*Griswold v. Connecticut*, 1965)	"Unless incriminating testimony is 'compelled,' any invasion of privacy is outside the scope of the Fifth Amendment's protection.... Accordingly, we hold that the search of an individual's office for business records, their seizure, and subsequent introduction into evidence do not offend the ... proscription that 'no person ... shall be compelled in any criminal case to be a witness against himself.' " (*Andersen v. Maryland*, 1976)

A Protection against Torture

"The establishment of the privilege is closely linked historically with the abolition of torture. Now we look upon torture with abhorrence. But torture was once used by honest and conscientious public servants as a means of obtaining information about crimes which could not otherwise be disclosed. We want none of that today." (Erwin N. Griswold, 1955)	"[The police officer] drew her gun and shot Martinez several times, causing severe injuries that left Martinez permanently blinded and paralyzed from the waist down.... Chavez accompanied Martinez to the hospital and then questioned Martinez there.... We find that Chavez's ... conduct did not violate the Self-Incrimination Clause." (*Chavez v. Martinez*, 2003)

THE PRIVILEGE AS SYMBOL	THE PRIVILEGE IN ACTION

Protection of the Innocent

"The privilege, while sometimes 'a shelter to the guilty,' is often 'a protection to the innocent.'" (*Murphy v. Waterfront Commission*, 1964)	"The basic purposes that lie behind the privilege against self-incrimination do not relate to protecting the innocent from conviction." (*Tehan v. United States*, 1966)
"The right to silence reduces the number of wrongful convictions." (Daniel J. Seidmann and Alex Stein, "*The Right to Silence Helps the Innocent: A Game-Theoretic Analysis of the Fifth Amendment Privilege*," 114 *Harvard Law Review*, no. 2 [Dec. 2000]: 503)	"[The privilege] derogates rather than improves the chances for accurate decisions." (*Baxter v. Palmigiano*, 1976)

Protecting the Dignity of the Individual

"The reprobation of compulsory self-incrimination is an established doctrine of our civilized society....A sense of personal degradation in being compelled to incriminate one's self must create a feeling of abhorrence in the community at its attempted enforcement." (*Brown v. Walker*, 1896, Justice Field dissenting)	"But even in the latter case, if the answer of the witness will not directly show his infamy, but only tend to disgrace him, he is bound to answer." (*Brown v. Walker*, 1896. Majority)

THE PRIVILEGE AS SYMBOL	THE PRIVILEGE IN ACTION

A Broad-Ranging Right

"[The privilege] can be asserted in any proceeding, civil or criminal, administrative or judicial, investigatory or adjudicatory; and it protects against any disclosures that the witness reasonably believes could be used in a criminal prosecution or could lead to other evidence that might be so used. This Court has been zealous to safeguard the values that underlie the privilege." (*Kastigar v. United States*, 1972)

"The Fifth Amendment privilege may not be invoked to resist compliance with a regulatory regime constructed to effect the State's public purposes unrelated to the enforcement of its criminal laws." (*Baltimore City Department of Social Services v. Bouknight*, 1990)

"Although Martinez contends that the meaning of 'criminal case' should encompass the entire criminal investigatory process, including police interrogations, we disagree. In our view, a 'criminal case' at the very least requires the initiation of legal proceedings." (*Chavez v. Martinez*, 2003)

At the Disposal of the Individual

"The Constitution...gives the defendant and his lawyer the absolute right to decide that the accused shall not become a witness against himself." (*Lakeside v. Oregon*, 1978)

"Where criminating facts have been voluntarily revealed, the privilege cannot be invoked to avoid disclosure of the details." (*Rogers v. United States*, 1951)

[98]

Many of the most powerful of these hortatory statements were made in the context of the abuses of McCarthyism. During the century and a half following the ratification of the Fifth Amendment, little was said about the importance of the right against self-incrimination. This should not be surprising, because an appreciation of rights often follows a recognition of wrongs. As I have argued elsewhere, rights change over time and place, but they do not change at a steady pace or in a symmetrical manner. Long periods of time pass with few or no changes. Then, suddenly, there is a burgeoning of new rights. My late colleague Stephen Jay Gould observed a phenomenon in nature that he called "punctuated equilibrium," pursuant to which evolutionary changes "happen in fits and starts." Though I am generally wary of using scientific observations of natural phenomena as metaphors for human inventions, there are some striking similarities between Gould's observations about evolution and my observations about rights. The history of rights shows long periods during which few changes seem to occur. Then a grievous human wrong, such as the Holocaust, suddenly takes place. The world eventually acknowledges the wrong and responds with a burgeoning of rights, as occurred following the Second World War, when international human rights took giant steps forward. Sometimes the wrong is not sudden, but rather of long duration, such as slavery. It is the recognition of the wrong—or its defeat after a conflict—that serves as a stimulus for the development of the right. The post–Civil War constitutional amendments quickly turned a right to own slaves into a right not to be owned as a slave.

There have also been some historical examples of rights quickly contracting in the aftermath of wrongs that were believed to be caused by excessive rights. We are now experiencing such a contraction in response to the terrorist attacks of recent years.

Both aspects of this phenomenon are apparent in the history of the privilege against self-incrimination, which has gone through cycles over time. It began as closely associated with religious and political rights. In nineteenth- and early twentieth-century America, the privilege was primarily a trial right. Then, with the advent of congressional investigations, culminating in the McCarthy era, its focus was largely on political investigations. Now it is once again primarily a trial right that is in danger of contraction because of the war on terrorism and the perceived need to employ coercion to secure preventive intelligence. Over time, the privilege has been understood, on one end of the continuum, as reflecting broad *political* rights of all persons and, on the other end of the continuum, as granting a narrow procedural trial *remedy* only to *criminal defendants* at their own trials.

The Supreme Court's majority in *Martinez* interpreted the privilege quite narrowly. The dissenters interpreted the privilege only slightly more broadly by recognizing a stand-alone right, enforceable by a damage remedy, not to be subject to "torture or its close equivalents." The dissenters apparently agreed that the privilege did not contain a stand-alone right not to be compelled by the threat of contempt or coercion (short of torture or its close equivalents) to make self-incriminating statements. After *Martinez*, the only Fifth Amendment right any person now has is the evidentiary remedy, *if* he becomes a *criminal defendant*, to exclude the fruits of the compulsion from his criminal trial.

Not a single justice endorsed a broader political right to remain silent or to keep the government out of any private or political enclave, as prior judicial and academic statements had suggested. To be sure, these broader aspects of the right were not specifically at issue in *Martinez*, but they were also not at issue in many of the cases in which justices have articulated the symbolic importance of the right. The disconnect between what courts have *said* about the right against self-incrimination and what they have *ruled* about that right raises questions that transcend the right against self-incrimination, questions regarding the general role of constitutional rights in our system of governance.

RIGHTS AS SPECIFIC LIMITATIONS ON PARTICULAR GOVERNMENTAL ACTIONS VERSUS RIGHTS AS GENERAL GUIDES TO GOVERNANCE

The Constitution, and especially the Bill of Rights, contains numerous provisions that have multiple meanings at varying levels of abstraction. They can be read quite narrowly as entrenching a particular right in a specific, often time-bound, context. But the same words can also be read quite broadly as enshrining a more general approach to governance. In a 1962 *Yale Law Journal* comment (which I had the privilege of editing), Professor John Hart Ely made this point with regard to an apparently obscure provision of the Constitution prohibiting any "bill of attainder" from being enacted by Congress or by state legislatures.

At one level, this prohibition could be read as merely disempowering legislatures from doing what the British Parliament had regularly done: enacting laws that sentenced traitors to death and "attainted" their blood without a judicial trial. Read so narrowly, the provision would have little, if any, current relevance, because our legislatures have not passed bills of attainder since the Revolution. To avoid such a dead-letter approach, some courts have given the clause a broader reading, interpreting it as forbidding "the *kinds* of evils" caused by traditional bills of attainder, even if the form is somewhat different. As the Supreme Court said in 1866: "If the [bill of attainder] inhibition can be evaded by the form of the enactment its insertion in the fundamental law was a vain and futile proceeding."

This "functional" approach—identifying "the *kinds* of evils" that were the focus of the framers and determining whether comparable evils are present in contemporary legislative actions— was employed by Chief Justice John Marshall as far back as 1810, when he suggested, in dictum, that the "bill of attainder" clause may prohibit not only laws that fall technically within that narrow category, but all legislatively imposed punishments that are inflicted without judicial trial.

Ely argued that the clause should be read even more broadly, as an important component of the separation of powers that serves as a structural protection against tyranny:

The dual rationale of the separation of powers—fear of over-concentration of power in any one branch, and a feeling that the various [branches are best] suited for different jobs—is reflected in the bill of attainder clause. Not only was there a general fear of legislative power on the part of the founding fathers, but there was also a specific realization that the legislative branch of government is more susceptible than the judiciary to such influences as passion, prejudice, personal solicitation, and political motives.... The bill of attainder clause is an implementation of their judgment that these factors render [it inappropriate for] the legislature ... to decide who comes within the purview of its general rules.... The bill of attainder clause, it is submitted, is a broad prohibition [that] tells legislatures that they may not apply their mandates to specific parties; they instead must leave the job of application to other tribunals.

Other scholars, and several courts, have disagreed with Ely's analysis, and this is not the place to debate its merits. I cite it merely to illustrate that constitutional provisions may legitimately bear both a narrow technical reading and a broader structural or symbolic reading.

Similar dichotomous readings have been accorded virtually every one of the provisions of the Bill of Rights. Many Americans understand the First Amendment, for example, to guarantee them a broad "right of free speech." But despite the common myth that we can say anything we please in this country, the fact is that our Bill of Rights does not grant Americans any general right of free speech. The First Amendment only prohibits federal (and now state) government actors from "abridging the freedom of speech, or of the press." The amendment, then, is a restriction on government power, not a right to say anything without fear of any consequences. The First Amendment says nothing about the power of private employers, universities, or sports leagues to censor or punish speakers who express views with which they disagree.

A similar analysis can be applied to the establishment clause of the First Amendment, which begins with the command that "Congress shall make no law...respecting an establishment of religion." The concept of establishing a religion had a specific, technical meaning in 1791, when several states had recent histories of selecting one particular Protestant sect—Anglicanism, Congregationalism, Baptism—as the "official" religion of the government. The established religion received governmental funding supported by the revenues raised from all tax-paying citizens, including members of other faiths that were "tolerated," at best, and discriminated against or even banned, at worst.

The narrow understanding of the establishment clause at the time of its ratification merely forbade the *federal* government from establishing one branch of Protestantism as the single official religion of the United States. It left each state free to establish a particular religion of its choice, or to establish none. Today, only extremists from the religious right would limit the establishment clause to its original narrow understanding. Even Justices Scalia and Thomas grudgingly acknowledge that the clause has been given a far broader interpretation by history and precedents.

Of course, there continues to be considerable controversy over the "proper" interpretation of the establishment clause, but even the narrowest current interpretation goes well beyond the specific prohibition that probably constituted the original understanding. The clause has become an important symbol of the separation of church and state—a phrase that does not even appear in the text of the Constitution.

Other aspects of the First Amendment—the free press, assembly, and petition provisions—also have both narrow technical and broader structural interpretations. At the broadest level, they—like the bill of attainder clause—can be viewed as part of our system of checks and balances. Not only does each *branch* of government check and balance the *other branches*, but nongovernmental institutions—media, the academy, religion, business—can serve as checks on government. As John Hart Ely wrote in his masterful book *Democracy and Distrust*, one of the important functions of the courts is to keep open the channels of democracy, which surely include all the institutions and practices protected by the First Amendment.

The Second Amendment is another illustration of a provision with both a narrow and a broad meaning. (In this instance, as contrasted with most others, it is generally conservatives who interpret its words broadly and liberals who interpret them narrowly.) The Amendment provides: "A well regulated Militia, being necessary to the security of a free State, the right of the people to keep and bear Arms, shall not be infringed."

The narrow reading, favored by gun control advocates, focuses on the initial clause and would limit the right to a *collective* one designed to preserve well-regulated state militias by prohibiting the federal government from disarming them. The broad reading, favored by gun advocates, focuses on the last clause and reads the initial words as merely hortatory. It would grant not only "the people" but each *individual* the right to own guns without infringement by the government. Charlton Heston, the president of the National Rifle Association, argued that the Second Amendment has a symbolic significance that transcends its words: "The Second Amendment must be considered more essential than the First Amendment.... The Second Amendment is...America's First Freedom, the one right that protects all the others.... It alone offers the absolute capacity to live without fear. The right to keep and bear arms is the one right that allows 'rights' to exist at all."

There are, of course, textual problems with the NRA's broad interpretation, as there are with the narrow interpretation. The Supreme Court, which has not yet provided a definitive interpretation of the Second Amendment, will be faced with a daunting challenge against the background of overheated political and ideological conflict. Part of this challenge will be whether to accord the amendment a narrow, technical, and time-bound interpretation or a broader, more functional, and contemporarily relevant construction.

The right against "excessive bail," contained in the Eighth Amendment, has long been thought by some to reflect a presumption of innocence that covers all citizens until they have been convicted of a crime, but the Supreme Court has recently ruled that there is no general presumption of innocence, merely an evidentiary rule that applies only in criminal trials. Similarly, the Eighth Amendment protection against "cruel and unusual punishments" was long believed to protect citizens against governmental abuse, such as torture, police beatings, and jailhouse violence. But the Supreme Court has ruled that the provision "was designed to protect" only those "convicted of crimes" and not as a more general prohibition against government abuse.

Other provisions of the Constitution have also been construed more broadly and symbolically (and sometimes more narrowly and literally) than their original understanding. These include the Fourth, Sixth, Eighth, Ninth, Tenth, Thirteenth, Fourteenth, Fifteenth, and Nineteenth Amendments.

SHOULD ANY PROVISIONS OF THE CONSTITUTION BE INTERPRETED SYMBOLICALLY?

Justice Scalia has argued that the words of the Constitution should not be interpreted broadly as the aspirational views of the framers, but narrowly as a codified catalogue of specific and limited rights. He articulated his position in response to a quite different approach proposed by Professor Lawrence Tribe:

> Professor Tribe describes these ... provisions as designed to "reflect[] ... the *aspirations* of the former colonists about what sorts of rights they and their posterity *would come to enjoy* against their own government" (emphasis added). I do not believe that. If you want aspirations, you can read the Declaration of Independence [or] the French Declaration of the Rights of Man. ... There is no such philosophizing in our Constitution, which ... is a practical and pragmatic charter of government. The aspirations of those who adopted it are set forth in its prologue—"to insure domestic Tranquility," among other things, and "to secure the Blessings of Liberty to ourselves and our Posterity." The operative provisions of the

document, on the other hand, including the Bill of Rights, abound in concrete and specific dispositions....

It would be most peculiar for aspirational provisions to be interspersed randomly among the very concrete and hence obviously nonaspirational prescriptions that the Bill of Rights contains—"jury trials in suits at common law for more than twenty dollars," followed by "all men are created equal," followed by "no quartering of troops in homes." It is more reasonable to think that the provisions are all of a sort. Professor Tribe emphasizes that such provisions as the guarantees of "the freedom of speech" and of "due process of law" are abstract and general rather than specific and concrete; but abstraction and generality do not equate with aspiration. The context suggests that the abstract and general terms, like the concrete and particular ones, are meant to nail down current rights, rather than aspire after future ones.

Scalia's illustrations—no quartering of troops, the twenty dollar criteria for civil trials—can of course be used to support the opposite conclusion: that the framers knew how to use narrow language when they wanted to. The fact that they used more open-ended language—precisely of the sort they knew common law courts would have to interpret over time—suggests that they may not necessarily have meant to "nail down" all rights, such as those mandating "equal protection," "due process," and the prohibition against "cruel and unusual punishments."

There is nothing "peculiar" or unusual for "aspirational provisions to be interspersed randomly among the very concrete... provisions." Random interspersion is typical of our Constitution, as illustrated by the placement of the right against self-incrimination in an amendment that covers the rights of *persons* rather than the rights of the *accused*. It is also typical of constitutions in general, as illustrated by Canada's Constitutional Act of 1982, which intersperses "the right to life, liberty, and security...in accordance with the principles of fundamental justice" with much more concrete rights. A similar mix of exhortation and technical statecraft can be found in the constitutions of France, Greece, South Africa, and elsewhere.

One obvious example in the Bill of Rights that undercuts Scalia's generalization that constitutional provisions were written "in concrete and specific dispositions" designed to "nail down" rights as they were understood at the time is the provision against double jeopardy that appears in the Fifth Amendment: "Nor shall any person be subject for the same offense to be twice put in jeopardy *of life or limb*" (emphasis added).

These twenty words have caused no end of interpretive litigation. The words "same offense" have divided judges bitterly over the years. Is it the "*same* offense" if all the *facts* are the same, and the same *crime* is prosecuted by the *federal* government and then by a *state*? Is it the "same offense" if the facts are the same but the "elements" of the crime are different?

And what about the words "life or limb"? Must they be interpreted literally? Now that many states have abolished capital punishment and all states have abolished corporal punishment, can any person ever be placed in jeopardy of his "life or limb" in these jurisdictions? Does the double jeopardy clause not apply to imprisonment? Can a person be subjected to a ten-year prison sentence and then tried again after he has served his term, since he was never literally placed in jeopardy of life or limb? Or should the words be read more generally to apply to *any* form of punishment?

Courts have been unanimous in interpreting these words expansively, despite the fact that punishments other than those jeopardizing lives and limbs were known to the framers, who were fully capable of "nailing" down the broader interpretation by using the word "punishments" in the double jeopardy clause as they did in the cruel and unusual punishments clause. Instead, they chose a somewhat literary, even poetic, formulation. A determined literalist would hold them to their choice of words and interpret the double jeopardy provision narrowly, as protecting against only the death penalty, ear cropping, and the like. But no court has done this, and with good reason. Justice Scalia has never provided a satisfactory explanation of why he would not read the clause literally, in accord with its supposed "original" understanding.

Phrases like "equal protection of the laws," "due process," "cruel and unusual punishments," "the freedom of speech," "secure in their persons," "speedy" trial, and "be a witness against himself" are also somewhat literary in their language. They too could have been "nailed down" by more technical formulations. But the framers selected more malleable, open-ended, vague, and symbolic phrases. What were future generations expected to make of that decision? What does the selection of these words—as distinguished from other, narrower and more technical words—tell us about the original understanding of the Bill of Rights? Or about how to construe such symbol-laden terms?

Professor Eben Moglen reminds us that the most basic right sought by the American colonists was "a constitutional right to the common law," which suggests a dynamic rather than a static constitutional law. They understood, as those who came after them understood, that it is a constitution, not a last will and testament, that courts would be expounding. As Professor Paul

Freund once put it, we must not "read the provisions of the Constitution like a last will and testament, lest indeed they become one."

The framers also understood that they were drafting an enduring charter of government that would be difficult to amend. As Alexander Hamilton wrote: "Constitutions should consist only of general provisions; the reason is that they must necessarily be permanent, and that they cannot calculate for the possible change of things." It doesn't sound as though he was seeking only to "nail down current rights."

In the end, our Constitution consists not *only* of general provisions; it contains some of the rather narrow particularistic provisions cited by Scalia, but it also contains more general provisions designed to assure the enduring nature of the document. Why the interpretive method that is appropriate for narrow technical and self-defining words (such as "twenty dollars," "thirty five years," and "a majority of those present") must be deemed equally appropriate for broad, symbolic, and common law terms, Scalia never explains. Henry Clay offered wiser counsel when he observed, "The Constitution of the United Sates was made not merely for the generation that then existed, but for posterity—unlimited, undefined, endless, perpetual posterity."

An enduring Constitution must balance between security and liberty, and that balance will inevitably vary with the current and enduring threats to each. Justice Jackson once warned, "If the Court does not temper its doctrinaire logic with a little practical wisdom, it will convert the constitutional Bill of Rights into a suicide pact." Justice Scalia seems to acknowledge—indeed, to welcome—the "last will and testament" and "suicide pact" approach, proudly describing the Constitution not as a "living document," but as a "dead" one, whose provisions have been "nail[ed] down" forever. This is an apt metaphor for a dead Constitution. He rejects Emily Dickinson's living approach to words:

> A word is dead
> When it is said,
> Some say.
> I say it just
> Begins to live
> That day.

Of course, Scalia argues that, if the Constitution, when read in this manner, does not serve the needs of the nation, then it should be amended or scuttled, not stretched by judges to fit the times. That, says Scalia, is the democratic way.

Ironically, this approach views constitutional interpretation through the prism of *modern* democracy, certainly post-Jacksonian democracy. But this was not the prism through which the framers understood the role of courts and judicial review. Many of the framers distrusted democracy, or "mobocracy" as some called it. They viewed the courts—composed of learned men appointed for life—as an essential elitist check on the people. They wanted to constitutionalize the common law, which would empower courts to interpret constitutional provisions without the need for repeated amendments or constitutional conventions. As Alexander Hamilton put it in *Federalist* no. 78, "the courts were designed to be an intermediate body between the people and the legislature, in order, among other things, to keep the latter within the limits assigned to their authority."

It is odd for Justice Scalia, of all people, to argue that the mode of interpretation most consistent with *modern* conceptions of democracy is to seek the original understanding of framers, who had *a very different* conception of democracy. As is so often the case with "originalists," he attributes to the framers his *own* views of the Constitution.

In fact, it is perfectly consistent with any reasonable concept of democracy, contemporary or eighteenth-century, to accept Hamilton's observation that the framers intended courts to have an "intermediate" role that checks and balances the authority assigned to the elected branches. And it is perfectly consistent with "democracy" for *some* constitutional provisions to be written in broad, symbolic terms, capable of expanding and contracting with the felt needs of the times, while others are written in narrow, inflexible terms. This seems a more accurate description of the original understanding of the framers than the crabbed one asserted, without proof, by Justice Scalia. It is a reading that helps to explain why our "accidental Constitution" has been so enduring.

OUR ACCIDENTAL CONSTITUTION

The Constitution, and its Bill of Rights, may have been intended for the ages—as Hamilton, Marshall, Clay, and others have attested—but it was also written in its time and for its time. That is inevitably the case with any document, regardless of how future-looking and farsighted it may have been. The frame of reference for our Constitution was late eighteenth-century, postrevolutionary America, a nation with slavery, male domination, Protestant sensibilities, and economic and other qualifications for voting, jury service, and office holding. Its frame of reference also included a criminal justice system that was relatively primitive, even by British standards. Trained lawyers were few; police, as we know them today, were nonexistent; professional prosecutors were rare; judges were often not well educated;

prisons for long-term confinement had not yet been constructed; alternatives to the death penalty were largely inefficient; and the parchment rights of criminal defendants were ignored in many cases.

It is remarkable that the Constitution—laden with regional and other compromises; hastily written; filled with drafting errors; combining time-bound, even anachronistic, provisions with broad, symbolic, and (arguably) aspirational words—has outlived all others, and with so few amendments. Part of the reason for this longevity is John Marshall's foresighted decisions that empowered the Courts to engage in judicial review: the power to declare the acts of other parts of the federal and state government unconstitutional. It is no accident that these decisions included the phrase "We must never forget, that it is a constitution we are expounding... a constitution intended to endure for ages to come, and, consequently, to be adapted to the various crises of human affairs."

Another part of the reason is that many of the Constitution's most important provisions were written in broad, flexible terms, capable of adaptation to changing times and circumstances. The adaptability of many of the Constitution's most important provisions, coupled with the difficulty of the amending process, has resulted in the text of the Constitution remaining largely the same, while taking on different meanings over time.

The Constitution today is a very different document from what it was in 1791, 1860, 1900, or 1950. Some of the difference is attributable to events and amendments. The most important of these are the Civil War, the post–Civil War amendments (the Thirteenth, Fourteenth, and Fifteenth), the massive immigration movements that began in the mid-nineteenth century and again in the post–World War II era, the depression and the New Deal, the enfranchisement of women, the resurrection of the moribund Bill of Rights during the twentieth century, the civil rights movement, and the Supreme Court's reapportionment and abortion decisions. The framers of our Constitution (even the most farsighted among them) would hardly recognize the way it has been "expounded" over the centuries.

Some of the reasons for the Constitution's adaptability have been largely accidental, a product of the law of unintended consequences. (In that respect, at least, it may be analogous to evolution.) The privilege against self-incrimination is a perfect example of accidental adaptability. At the time the Fifth Amendment was ratified, according to Langbein and others, the privilege was rarely invoked by criminal defendants at their trials. Its words could not have been understood to mean what the "defendant's privilege" means today, because defendants were *disqualified* from testifying under oath whether they wanted to or not. It is not entirely clear, therefore, what the privilege was understood to mean in the context of the eighteenth-century model of the criminal trial.

Although its words, literally read, would appear to apply only to a criminal defendant not being compelled to be a witness against himself at his own trial, Professor Donald Dripps has astutely observed that such an understanding would "confine the privilege to the only context in which it was unavailable at the founding." Today, the privilege has been given a meaning that makes sense in the context of our modern system of criminal justice in which, absent the privilege, the defendant could be called as a witness by either side, as he can in a civil case. But it was not the plan of the framers to draft words that would eventually make sense in a system that they did not envision. It is largely an accident that the words of the privilege fit comfortably into our current adversarial trial.

Not all provisions have fared as well against the contingencies of history. The Third Amendment's prohibition against the quartering of troops has become an anachronism, and efforts to interpret it as metaphor for the privacy of the home have fallen largely on deaf ears. The Seventh Amendment's financial criteria for jury trial in civil cases at common law—twenty dollars—has trivialized the right, because what was a considerable sum in 1791 is now less than the filing fee.

It is uncertain how other provisions will fare. For example, the Second Amendment may well have been understood by the framers (or at least some of them) to be limited to "well-regulated militias," but its words are open to a broader interpretation, bestowing a generalized individual "right to bear arms." This has given rise to a large and powerful political movement that can point to some of the words of that amendment as its justification. This "right to bear arms" movement has in turn given rise to a countermovement favoring gun control that points to other words, such as "well-regulated," as its justification. That dispute has yet to be resolved by the Supreme Court.

Another "accidental" provision of the Constitution is the "due process" clause. No framer ever imagined that this procedural guarantee would take on a substantive meaning that would extend to protecting economic rights, gay rights, abortion rights, and grandparental rights. Justice Scalia doesn't regard these adaptations as accidental, but rather as deliberate, political, perverse, and antidemocratic.

Regardless of how one assesses this issue, there can be little dispute about the conclusion that many of the Constitution's most important words and phrases have significantly different meanings today than they did when originally written, and that many of these differences have been the result of accident. But this observation does not answer the question whether the right against self-incrimination, or any other constitutional right, should be interpreted in accord with its broad, symbolic understanding, or limited to its narrower, more technical application. Should it be construed functionally, rather than literally? It is to this question that we now turn.

CHAPTER SEVEN

The Relevance of Constitutional Policies
Underlying the Right

A FUNCTIONAL ANALYSIS OF THE PRIVILEGE
AGAINST SELF-INCRIMINATION

In addition to viewing certain constitutional provisions in a symbolic manner, courts sometimes apply provisions functionally. John Hart Ely defined the functional approach as one that "interprets a Constitutional provision in light of the sort of evil against which it was directed. It thus might perhaps be termed 'historical functionalism.' "

A historically functional analysis of a constitutional right is different from a policy analysis of that right. A functional analysis must be rooted in the historic policies underlying the right. It interprets these policies by reference to what the *framers* understood to be the evils addressed by the constitutional provision, and not by reference to the values and policies of the *current interpreters*. To be sure, there is always the danger that a functional analysis will serve merely as a cover for a policy evaluation, allowing interpreters to slip their own policy preferences into the mix, but this risk is present with *any* mode of constitutional analysis, whether textual, precedential, analogical, or historical.

A functional analysis must begin, as must all modes of interpretation, with the text and history of the provision. Its goal is to identify the wrongs sought to be righted by the provision. If these wrongs persist, perhaps in somewhat different forms, then a functional analysis will further the original understanding of the framers.

In his opinion for the Court in *Hudson v. Michigan* (2006), Justice Scalia purported to employ a functional analysis in deciding whether a violation of the "knock and announce" requirement of the Fourth Amendment warranted application of the exclusionary rule. He (along with Justices Thomas, Kennedy, Roberts, and Alito) ruled that the exclusionary rule is inapplicable when the police, with a search warrant, fail to satisfy the knock and announce requirement. He acknowledged that this "ancient" requirement has "its origins in our English legal heritage" and is "a command of the Fourth Amendment." But he invoked several recent developments to justify his conclusion that the cost of applying the exclusionary rule in this situation outweighs the benefits.

Among the developments he invoked was the availability of a tort remedy under 42 U.S.C. §1983, a remedy that he said is experiencing a "slow but steady expansion." It was, of course, precisely this remedy that the Court, with his agreement, denied to Oliverio Martinez just three years earlier. Another change he pointed to is "the increasing professionalism of police forces"—a change not evident in the behavior of the police toward Martinez. In the light of such developments, Scalia concluded that the Court "cannot assume that exclusion in this context is necessary deterrence simply because we found that it was necessary deterrence in different contexts" in the past. (By contrast, in *Martinez*, Justice

Scalia apparently concluded that exclusion is sufficient deterrence in the context of torture or other coercive mechanisms for eliciting compelled self-incriminatory statements.)

Scalia's dynamic approach to constitutional interpretation in *Hudson*—as circumstances change, so too must constitutional interpretation change—fits more comfortably into the "living Constitution" school of thought that Scalia eschews than to the "dead Constitution" school of which he is the dean. In *Hudson*, Scalia conveniently employed the kind of functional approach and cost-benefit analysis that he usually condemns as more appropriate for legislators than for judges. Conveniently, a functional analysis brings Scalia to his preferred policy outcome in *Hudson*, just as the opinion in *Martinez*, which he joined, brought him to his preferred policy outcome by eschewing a functional analysis.

Let us consider, then, how such a functional approach, invoked by Scalia in *Hudson* but rejected in *Martinez*, might have informed the decision in *Martinez*.

THE POLICIES UNDERLYING THE PRIVILEGE

Over the years, courts and commentators have articulated many constitutional policies that are thought to underlie the right against compelled self-incrimination. These policies fall into several categories. The first relates to the *unreliability* of self-incriminating statements secured by coercion. As far back as the twelfth century, Maimonides worried that suicidal individuals might falsely confess, even voluntarily, in order to secure the assistance of the legal system in ending their lives. Coerced confessions are even more suspect, and those obtained through the use of torture are the least reliable because some people may say almost anything to stop being tortured.

In the *Martinez* case, for example, the self-incriminating statements elicited from Martinez while he was seeking medical relief from excruciating pain and the likelihood of imminent death, might well have been false. After repeatedly saying that he didn't know exactly what happened, Martinez finally responded "yes" to the police officer's question whether he pointed the gun at another officer. In light of his serious wounds, it is certainly possible that he did not remember precisely what happened and in what order. Perhaps he did and was telling the truth, but one cannot be certain based on the circumstances surrounding the interrogation. This is one reason this admission would have been excluded from his criminal trial had he been prosecuted.

Here, it may be useful to compare and contrast interrogating an individual to secure admissible evidence of past crimes with which to *prosecute* him with interrogating an individual in order to elicit *preventive* intelligence. The similarities are largely moral in nature and relate to issues of bodily integrity, autonomy, dignity, and privacy. They are also legal, because many treaties, conventions, and statutes prohibit certain interrogation techniques without regard to the purpose of the interrogation. A strong case can be made for prohibiting torture without regard to the accuracy or inaccuracy of the resulting information, because torture is thought to be per se morally and legally offensive. Other forms of coercive interrogation, such as those involving threats, promises, tricks, discomfort, even "truth serum," might also be deemed per se morally unacceptable, at least in the context of eliciting evidence of past crimes for use against a criminal defendant. But the same might not be true in the preventive intelligence situation.

The differences between the two types of interrogation are a combination of empirical, moral, and legal. They relate largely to the accuracy and value of the information elicited and the importance of the state's interest in obtaining the information. One critical difference may be in the ratio of false positives to false negatives deemed acceptable and lawful in eliciting *evidence* for criminal *prosecution*, as distinguished from *intelligence* for use in *preventing* acts of terrorism or other extremely harmful *future* crimes.

Assume that a particular form of interrogation—say, water boarding—produces truthful information 25 percent of the time and false information 75 percent of the time. Assume further that the accuracy of the information cannot be definitively corroborated by external evidence (such as DNA, fingerprints, etc.) and must therefore be considered alone for its truth or falsity. We would be hesitant to admit such probably inaccurate and prejudicial evidence against a criminal defendant at his trial. The principle that it is better for ten guilty defendants to go free than for even one innocent defendant to be falsely convicted would militate against admitting such evidence, especially because jurors tend to place heavy reliance on "confessions" of guilt. A system that came to rely on such evidence would likely produce the conviction of many innocent (as well as some guilty) defendants.

Contrast this, however, to the use of such information in preventive intelligence gathering: any intelligence agency in the world would be delighted to have relevant, real-time information that is accurate 25 percent of the time. The "precautionary principle" employs a very different ratio of false positives to false negatives, especially when the preventive action to be taken is less intrusive than a criminal conviction—for example, clearing a building, increasing security, diverting aircraft, detaining a suspect, searching a home or a computer. The more intrusive the preventive measure, the higher the ratio of truth to falsity should be required in the interest of preventing a given threat. This calculus can, of course, become quite complex: as the gravity of the risk increases—for example, an imminent nuclear attack versus a roadside bomb—the required ratio of truth to falsity will decrease in the context of any particular preventive measure. But if the *risk* and the *intrusion both* increase, the necessary ratio of false positives to false negatives will be subject to reasonable disagreement, based on both empirical and moral grounds.

This is all merely intended to demonstrate that the policy considerations may differ greatly depending on the use to which the information elicited by questionable interrogation methods is to be put. Based on these factors, one might also draw distinctions within the paradigm of eliciting evidence for use against a criminal defendant at his trial. For example, a confession that leads the police to indisputable physical evidence of guilt of murder might be treated differently from an uncorroborated confession that provides only marginally probative evidence of guilt of theft. (More about this later.)

The best evidence that unreliability is not the only concern undergirding the right against compelled self-incrimination is that even completely reliable compelled admissions are excluded from evidence under the privilege. This may reflect broader unreliability concerns (based on "rule" rather than "case" utilitarianism)—namely, that a system that relies on compelled self-incrimination will produce too many unreliable admissions over time, and the best way to prevent that from happening is a wholesale rule that does not attempt to distinguish on a case-by-case basis between unreliable and reliable compelled statements. The broad exclusionary rule may also be designed to reduce the frequency of certain abusive interrogation techniques without regard to whether they tend to produce reliable or unreliable information.

This leads to the second reason that evidence of compelled confession is excluded: to disincentivize the police from employing certain interrogation techniques. One judicial mechanism for discouraging abusive methods of interrogation is the exclusionary rule. It is possible that the framers of the Fifth Amendment opted for exclusion as the exclusive mechanism for eliminating torture and other forms of coercion. This seems unlikely, however, in the face of the history of the Fifth Amendment and the very different language of the Fourth Amendment, which does not include an exclusionary rule.

The courts have created an exclusionary rule as one of the mechanisms to enforce the prohibitions of the Fourth Amendment. Some of the same justices who most strongly disfavor the exclusionary rule in the context of the Fourth Amendment strongly favor it as the *exclusive* remedy in the context of the Fifth Amendment. This is understandable in light of the different language and formulations of the two amendments: the Fourth Amendment articulates a primary right of persons to be free of "unreasonable searches and seizures," without specifying a particular remedy for violations of the right, whereas the Fifth Amendment could plausibly be interpreted to specify a very particular *remedy* for the improper use of compulsion in criminal cases.

Whereas judicial creativity was necessary to create an *exclusionary* remedy for "unreasonable searches and seizures," such creativity (or legislation) would be necessary to create a *damages* remedy for the improper use of compulsion in criminal cases. Thus, those who favor judicial restraint over judicial creativity— without regard to the substance of the issue involved—can plausibly oppose a Fourth Amendment exclusionary rule while also opposing a judicially created Fifth Amendment damages remedy. That this set of outcomes, narrowing the remedies available under both amendments, would be attributable, according to this view, to the framers, not to the courts.

But was this really the intention or understanding of the framers, or is it merely a consequence of inartful language and careless placement of the rights? Did the framers affirmatively intend the fruits of unlawful searches under the Fourth Amendment to be admitted into evidence against criminal defendants and for the only remedy to be damage suits? Did they affirmatively intend the fruits of coerced statements to be excluded from evidence against criminal defendants and for noncriminal defendants to have no remedy against those who coerce or even torture them? As a matter of common sense, this seems unlikely.

The relationship between the Fourth and Fifth Amendments has been a subject of considerable controversy from the very beginning, as reflected in Chief Justice Marshall's ruling in the *Burr* case that "no man can be forced to furnish *evidence* against himself" (emphasis added), which apparently included *physical* evidence, such as the document at issue in that case. It is possible that the framers did not explicitly include an exclusionary remedy in the Fourth Amendment because they believed (as Marshall apparently did) that the Fifth Amendment itself provided such a remedy against at least some violations of the Fourth Amendment. But that belongs in the realm of unanswerable historical speculation.

The Fourth Amendment exclusionary rule has long been a source of controversy because it is considered a "guilty man's remedy." That may be an apt characterization of the rule in the context of the Fourth Amendment, because physical evidence is generally reliable, even if it is unlawfully secured. But in the context of compelled or coerced confessions, the excluded evidence is often of questionable accuracy. Its exclusion could therefore benefit innocent as well as guilty persons.

Moreover, the mechanisms underlying exclusionary rules are often misunderstood. Although the courts often refer to *deterrence* as the object of exclusionary rules, that is a misuse of the term. For a sanction to *deter* an activity, the costs of the sanction must exceed the benefits of the activity. For example, a bank robber who expects to net $100,000 will not be deterred by a threatened sanction of having to return the $100,000 in the event of a conviction.

A threatened sanction of $200,000 might deter him if the likelihood of getting caught and convicted is higher than 50 percent. A long prison term would deter him even more effectively if it is a near certainty. A threatened sanction of $100,000 might reduce his incentive to rob the bank (relative to a world in which he faces no sanction), but it hardly counts as "deterrence."

So too with an exclusionary rule. If such a remedy does no more than put the police in the same situation they would have been in absent the violation of law, such a remedy could *disincentivize* but not *deter*. For the law violation to be deterred would require a credible threat of sanctions that exceed in expected cost the expected benefits of the violation. A damages action *in addition* to the exclusion remedy might actually *deter* the violation.

A functional approach to constitutional interpretation does not point unerringly in one direction in the context of the question before the Court in *Martinez*. Although *one* of the evils to which the right against self-incrimination was directed was surely torture (or torture-like coercion), the historical evidence is unclear as to whether the framers sought to address this evil by only *one* constitutional remedy: exclusion of the evidence (and its fruits) in criminal cases. A mirror-image uncertainty exists with regard to the Fourth Amendment, which on its face provides no exclusionary remedy. A functional analysis of the Fourth Amendment led the Court to add an exclusionary remedy, but the Court in *Martinez* refused to add a damages remedy to the Fifth Amendment's exclusionary rule.

CHAPTER EIGHT

. . .

A Matter of Interpretation

How, then, should an intellectually honest justice committed to nonideological interpretation of the Constitution go about construing a provision, such as the privilege against self-incrimination, when after a thorough analysis, she comes to the following conclusions?

1. The text is subject to multiple, reasonable interpretations, some of which appear too narrow and some too broad to fit the precedents. The text alone does not point unerringly to a particular result.
2. The precedents are not directly on point, but could sustain multiple plausible interpretations, none of which is compelled or excluded by the precedents.
3. Analogies are incomplete, flawed, or cut in multiple directions. No analogy to established law or practice leads inexorably to one interpretation.

4. The original understanding leads to no single interpretation because the framers did not address the particular issue. Although language among the framers could support several plausible interpretations, their actual understanding is inaccessible. There is historical support for the conclusion that the framers understood the privilege to prohibit judicial torture and judicial oaths, but there is no definitive evidence of their understanding with regard to remedies.

5. Because the current system of criminal justice is so different from the various systems in place at the founding, it is difficult to extrapolate confidently from the historical understandings to the present situation.

6. A review of the understanding of the privilege, especially its symbolic power over the generations, would not support limiting it to a technical trial remedy available only to criminal defendants.

7. More recent understandings of the privilege have varied with the climate of the times and the nature of the "wrongs"—such as McCarthyism, on the one hand, and the freeing of guilty defendants, on the other—that have been most salient in any particular era.

8. Functional considerations of constitutional policy cut both ways depending on one's political, ideological, and other preferences. Considering the text at different levels of abstraction suggests different answers, but there is no definitive guide to the proper level of abstraction. Functional considerations also depend on an empirical assessment of how different constitutional policies might affect such issues as the use of torture in terrorist prevention efforts, the international law and treaty obligations of the United States, and other often contentious contemporary concerns.

9. Other modes of constitutional interpretation that have been employed by courts and advocated by scholars fail to produce a satisfactory singular result that does not appear to be more than a cover for ideological and political preferences.

Unlike some other constitution makers, the framers of our Constitution did not incorporate in the text a single proper mode or modes of interpretation. Nor has the Supreme Court embraced a definitive canon of constitutional construction. In this state of the law, an interpreter must decide which modes of interpretation to employ. That decision, and the theory on which it is based, should be clearly articulated, subjected to accountability and criticism, and consistently applied.

There are several kinds of theories of interpretation. Some purport to be deontological, that is, morally compelled without regard to consequences. Others are consequentialist, based on assumptions about costs and benefits. Some have elements of both, containing normative rules that depend to some degree on empirical assumptions.

To the extent that a theory of interpretation is based on consequentialist or utilitarian considerations, it should contain testable propositions that are subject to validation and invalidation. They should include null hypotheses.

Several techniques of invalidation have widespread, if often implicit, acceptance. One of these techniques purports to test any proposed theory of constitutional interpretation against a handful of *constitutionally given results*. If the particular theory of interpretation would not have led to these results without doing violence to its methodology, it fails the test—or at least, it must acknowledge that it is an imperfect theory of interpretation. (Even an imperfect theory can be accepted if it is less imperfect than the others.) The primary testing result, under this technique, is *Brown v. Board of Education* (1954). Under this test, it is taken as a given (although this wasn't always the case) that legally mandated racial segregation of public schools must be unconstitutional. Any credible theory of constitutional interpretation must require the striking down of such segregation—despite the fact that virtually all of the framers of the Fourteenth Amendment did not understand or affirmatively *intend* that amendment to prohibit the racial segregation of schools. Some of the most creative (and convoluted) intellectual (and sophistic) efforts have been undertaken by scholars to square this circle.

The two extreme views of constitutional interpretation are easy to state. The first, the strict "originalist" approach, acknowledges that there is no way to reconcile the text of the Fourteenth Amendment, as the framers understood its words, with judicially mandated desegregation of the schools. It therefore concludes that *Brown* was wrong as a matter of constitutional interpretation, (though perhaps understandable, maybe even justifiable, as a matter of pragmatic realpolitik). Under this view, a constitutional amendment (or at least legislation) was constitutionally required if the nation was to outlaw the racial segregation of schools. That neither could possibly have succeeded, especially with the malapportioned legislatures of 1954, does not concern the advocates of this view of constitutional interpretation. In their view, democracy requires the people themselves to make these decisions, unless the text of the Constitution, as understood by its framers, mandates a different result. This is the position Justices Scalia and Thomas *should* take on *Brown*, if they are principled in their adherence to their version of strict "originalism," but I am not aware they have done so.

The other extreme approach is the so-called expanding or living Constitution. This view acknowledges that the framers themselves understood "the equal protection of the laws" as allowing racial segregation and, indeed, that many, if not most, of the framers would not have voted for the amendment had they suspected that it would one day be used to strike down segregation. But the proponents of this approach maintain that the intent of the framers is largely irrelevant to constitutional interpretation, unless the text of the Constitution unequivocally requires an otherwise "unacceptable" result—which it rarely does. The job of the Court is to keep the Constitution relevant to changing times, conditions, and attitudes. So long as the words of the Constitution will plausibly bear an interpretation that keeps it relevant and vibrant, that interpretation should govern, regardless of the history or the original understanding, intent, or meaning of the text.

Another technique of invalidation is the one often cited by Justice Scalia (and previously cited by Justice Black). It demands that any proposed mode of interpretation deny justices the power to impose their own personal, political, religious, or ideological views on the decision-making process. Antonin Scalia worried aloud during his confirmation hearing whether his decisions reflect "the most fundamental, deeply felt beliefs of our society, which is what a Constitution means, [or whether] I am reflecting the most deeply felt beliefs of Scalia, which is not what I want to impose on the society." The Supreme Court's decision in *Bush v. Gore* (2000) demonstrates—if any demonstration is necessary—that no methodology of judicial review will prevent determined justices from imposing their own views on the Constitution (even if for one case only).

A variation on the above stated approach is one that eschews balancing in favor of absolute prohibitions. This too purports to limit the power of judges to smuggle their values into the judicial act of striking the "proper" constitutional balance. Justice Hugo Black insisted that the words of the First Amendment, "Congress shall make *no* law...abridging the freedom of speech..."

(emphasis added), had to be interpreted literally and absolutely to prohibit *any* and *all* restrictions on freedom of speech. It is, of course, impossible to apply such an absolute approach to all verbal utterances, including the offering of bribes, the solicitations of crimes, the planning of conspiracies, and other forms of traditionally prohibited statements. So Justice Black was quick to assert that many such forms of expression—for example, the wearing of a jacket in court that had the words "Fuck the Draft" written on it, as well as some union signs that were parts of labor pickets—were simply not "speech," within the meaning of the First Amendment. Some have accused Justice Black of sophistry or even intellectual dishonesty, while others have supported his absolutist approach as a useful tactic, designed to make it more difficult to impose restrictions on the freedom of speech. Reasonable people can and do disagree over whether this "absolutist" tactic is preferable to a more candid acknowledgment of the absence of absolutes in the real world, where all rights are necessarily relative and subject to reasonable restrictions and limitations.

No one mode of constitutional interpretation, and indeed no combination of modes, will inexorably lead to the "right" constitutional result in the face of textual and historical ambiguity. One thing that seems clear to me, though I know there is some dispute even with regard to it, is that judges have a responsibility to be candid, honest, and open about the absence of a single "right" answer and an obligation to explain why, in light of the availability of multiple plausible answers, they chose a particular one. Too few justices are as open as they should be about these ambiguities, uncertainties, and choices. Most prefer a *Wizard of Oz* approach, pretending that they are oracles whose role it is to *discover*, rather than to *invent* or *construct*, the "constitutionally mandated" outcome. They seem to think it is important for the public to believe that there is only one right result.

[131]

Moreover, the view that every issue that is not unambiguously and unequivocally resolved by the Constitution should necessarily be left to the democratic process is unsustainable. The challenge of constitutional interpretation cannot properly be resolved by invoking such a preference for democratic over judicial decision making. This was simply not the original understanding or intent of the framers, many of whom distrusted democracy and saw the judiciary as an essential check on intolerant, oppressive, and impatient majorities. Those who advocate the democratic resolution of issues that might reasonably be resolved by constitutional decision often fail to mention the undemocratic composition of the original electorate (male, landowning, white) and the limited role the electorate played in electing the president, senators, and other policy makers. They view the issue through the prism of *modern* democracy, while purporting to view it through the prism of the *framers*.

In a case like *Martinez*, the Court must interpret the Constitution as honestly and objectively as possible, openly employing acceptable canons of interpretation. One such canon, implicitly employed by some justices, favors a broad and expanding view of constitutional rights. Liberals such as Justices William Brennan, Arthur Goldberg, Earl Warren, and Ruth Bader Ginsburg have argued in favor of a "living" Constitution whose rights are capable of being expanded beyond their original narrow purview. Justice Ginsburg has observed that an important part of our history "is the story of the *extension* of constitutional rights and protections to people once ignored or excluded." Professor Lawrence Tribe insists that our living Constitution "invites us, and our judges, *to expand* on the panoply of freedoms that are uniquely part of our heritage." These liberals see the Constitution as "evolving"—that is, moving toward *more* liberty, *more* equality, and *more* due process. They fear that the opposite trend will move us backward toward a "stagnant, archaic, hidebound document steeped in the prejudices and superstitions of a time long past." Nor do they agree with those who claim that a "dead" Constitution will "depoliticize" or limit the power of the judiciary in an ideologically neutral manner. As Justice Brennan has argued:

> The political underpinnings of such a choice should not escape notice. A position that upholds constitutional claims only if they were within the specific contemplation of the Framers in effect establishes a presumption of resolving textual ambiguities against the claim of constitutional right. It is far from clear what justifies such a presumption.... Nothing intrinsic in the nature of interpretation—if there is such a thing as the "nature" of interpretation—commands such a passive approach to ambiguity. This is a choice no less political than any other; it expresses antipathy to claims of the minority... against the majority. Those who would restrict claims of right to the values... specifically articulated in the Constitution turn a blind eye to social progress and eschew adaptation of overarching principles to changes of social circumstance.

In other words, the liberals acknowledge that their preferred mode of interpreting the "living" Constitution serves to *expand* rights, because they see the Constitution as an "evolving" document that moves in one direction. According to at least some of them, it is a ratchet that locks movement only in the forward position: toward more liberty, equality, due process. They insist that the conservatives' preferred mode of interpretation serves to *contract* rights by limiting them to "the standards that prevailed in 1685 when Lord Jeffreys presided over the Bloody Assizes." According to this view, the conservative approach is anything but neutral. It reflects outmoded views of limited rights that just happen to correspond largely with the ideological preferences of those who claim to be bound by *their* version of the original understanding.

This description is generally accurate. Most contemporary justices and scholars who advocate a living Constitution are, in fact, liberals whose personal perspectives favor an expansive, evolving approach to constitutional rights. And most of those who advocate a dead Constitution are, in fact, conservatives whose personal perspectives favor a narrowing of constitutional rights.

But these general observations do not provide definitive guidance about how to decide particular issues or specific cases. They don't tell us *which* rights are properly subject to expansion over time, or by what criteria we should distinguish dynamic from static provisions. Liberals advocate a broad conception of the First Amendment when it comes to sexual expression, but not when it comes to commercial advertising or corporate speech. Conservatives advocate a broad conception of the First Amendment for corporate speech and commercial advertising, but not necessarily when it comes to sexual expression. Liberals advocate a broad conception of the equal protection clause when it comes to gay rights, but not when it comes to race-specific affirmative action. Conservatives advocate a broad conception of the equal protection clause when it comes to race-specific affirmative action, but not when it comes to sexual orientation. Is the Second Amendment's guarantee of the right to bear arms "dynamic" or "static"? And so on.

One of the most brilliant judges in the world, former president Aharon Barak of the Israeli Supreme Court, who has written extensively on the art of judicial interpretation, has argued that in close "cases in which a judge has discretion that allows him to choose among a limited number of options," he must

> choose the solution that seems to him the best accommodation of the competing purposes he or she has considered. Within

this scope, pragmatism operates. My advice is that, at this stage of the interpretive activity, the judge should aspire to achieve justice. This means justice for the parties before the court and with regard to the whole legal system. Justice guides the entire interpretive process, for, indeed, justice is one of the core values of the legal system. Within the bounds of judicial discretion, justice becomes a "residual" value which can decide hard cases. Of course, it is only natural that different judges have different conceptions of justice, for justice is a complex concept. Despite all its theoretical complexity, however, each of us has an intuitive feeling about the just solution of a dispute. This feeling must guide us at all stages of the interpretive process. It must direct our decisions in hard cases, when judicial discretion becomes our most essential tool.

The canons of interpretation selected—and omitted—by Justice Thomas in *Martinez* did not seem to include this important "residual value." Nor do they assign an appropriate burden of proof or persuasion to those who would expand or contract justice, rights, liberty, or other transcendent values. Instead, Thomas employed selective textualism, selective use of precedent, and questionable use of analogy to interpret the privilege against self-incrimination as not protecting a right to recover damages for coercive interrogations by the police—indeed, as not even prohibiting torture. He eschewed all references to history or original understanding, despite his frequent resort to such interpretive tools in other cases. Had he looked honestly to history and original understanding, he would have had a far more difficult time justifying the narrow interpretation he gave to the privilege, limiting it to an exclusionary rule without regard to the nature or degree of the coercion.

In the end, the decision in *Martinez* may have reflected the justices' policy preferences, both those in the majority and those in dissent. But those preferences went largely unexpressed and un-revealed. Moreover, the justices—none of whom is experienced in the area of the law in which the privilege plays an important role—are not particularly well qualified to make policy choices regarding self-incrimination. These choices, as we shall see in the conclusion, should be based on complex factors, many of which are largely inaccessible to the justices.

The Case for a Vibrant Privilege in the Preventive State

IN LIGHT OF MY CONCLUSION that none of the traditional modes of constitutional construction leads unerringly in the direction of the result reached by the Court in *Martinez*, and the likelihood that its holding was more a reflection of the policy preference of the justices than the principled constraints of constitutional interpretation, it is appropriate for me to end this book with my own observations about the enduring importance of the privilege against self-incrimination in the preventive state.

The preventive state seeks to anticipate and stop harms before they occur. The threat of mass-casualty suicide terrorism is pushing democratic societies, and especially those most vulnerable to this threat, away from exclusive reliance on a deterrence or punitive model and toward a more preventive model. Suicide terrorism cannot be deterred by democracies committed to the principle of individual guilt and prohibited from punishing the innocent relatives or friends of suicide terrorists. Accordingly, these nations are developing options that are designed to detect and stop terrorists (and other serious harm-doers) before they can act.

In the preventive state, coercion will be increasingly employed against individuals in order to secure *intelligence information* believed necessary to prevent future crimes, rather than to secure *evidence* of past crimes for use in criminal trials. As former attorney general John Ashcroft announced shortly after the terrorist attacks of September 11, 2001, the "number one priority" of the Justice Department is "prevention." An important element in this effort is the gathering of intelligence information by means that include coercive interrogation that would clearly result in the exclusion of its fruits in a criminal case against the coerced defendant.

Following the decision in *Martinez*, the privilege has no application to such preventive coercion, so long as its fruits are not used against the coerced person at his own criminal trial. This is part of a larger problem about which I have a written elsewhere—namely, the presence of a gaping black hole in the area of preventive intrusions and the absence of a clear jurisprudence to fill that gap.

This problem has become especially acute in the context of coercive interrogations since *Martinez*. Before we turn to that problem, however, let us consider the general policies underlying more traditional applications of the privilege in the context of interrogations calculated to produce confessions and other evidence for use in ordinary criminal cases. We will thus be better equipped to extrapolate from the limits the courts have placed on evidentiary interrogation to the limits, if any, they should place on preventive intelligence interrogation.

POLICIES UNDERLYING THE PRIVILEGE

It has become a staple of academic literature to criticize the privilege against self-incrimination, to argue that it serves no contemporary purpose, and to call for its abolition or limitation. Perhaps the most prominent critic of the privilege in the post-McCarthy era was Judge Henry Friendly, who called for a constitutional amendment to limit the privilege in important ways. In a series of lectures, Friendly summarized the extensive academic literature critical of the privilege:

> Wigmore... urged that the privilege "be kept within limits the strictest possible." In language which seems odd today he said of some relatively mild decisions of that era that they had so extended the privilege "as almost to be incredible, certainly to defy common sense."...
>
> Moving 30 years forward, Professor E. S. Corwin, the dean of constitutional commentators, was certain in 1930 that what he deemed the then erroneously expanded privilege "will in the immediate future undergo curtailment rather than extension." In 1934, Dean Roscoe Pound condemned the privilege as a device which serves not the innocent, but rather the evil purposes of criminals.... Three years later Mr. Justice Cardozo... made the famous remarks that immunity from compulsory self incrimination "might be lost, and justice still be done" and that "justice would not perish if the accused were subject to a duty to respond to orderly inquiry."
>
> Professor Edmund M. Morgan [wrote] in 1942 that "The extent to which the privilege against self-incrimination should be continued is worth extended study by thoughtful men."... Four years later another wise and moderate scholar, Professor McCormick, expressed the hope "that the courts as they become more conversant with the history of the privilege will see that it is a survival that has outlived the context that gave it meaning."

Friendly acknowledged that the privilege had served the nation well during the McCarthy era and played an important role in preserving political and religious liberty during earlier periods of repression, but he argued that by the 1960s it stood in the way of convicting murderers, kidnappers, and other "real" criminals. For Friendly there were the "good" criminals of yesteryear—the John Lilburnes and other religious and political dissidents—and the "bad" criminals of his day, who were hiding behind the privilege to get away with murder. Listen to Friendly's critique of the privacy rationale underlying the privilege:

> Far from being a moral doctrine, the privacy justification is about as immoral as one could imagine. To be sure, there may be offenses, for example, fornication and adultery, where the individual's right to be let alone may transcend the state's interest in solving them. Also, the privacy consideration has real application when a witness is being interrogated about associations and beliefs, but that ... is [not what] generally arises. How can it be seriously argued that when a murder or rape or kidnapping has been committed, a citizen is morally justified in withholding his aid simply because he ... prefers to remain in a "private enclave" from which the state has cause to believe he departed in order to do violence to another?

Friendly expressed a rather different view of the privilege in the context of the First Amendment:

> "In its origins, [the privilege] ... was associated then with guilt for crimes of conscience, of belief, and of association. In the broadest sense it was a protection not of the guilty, or of the innocent, but of freedom of expression, of political liberty, of the right to worship as one pleased." This is the privilege we

love. Here [the] eloquence on privacy rings true, as it does not
in the case of the murderer, the rapist or the bagman.

It would be tempting to suggest that Friendly did not understand that the law cannot easily distinguish good from bad criminals in devising rules of general applicability. Virtually every rule
that serves as a shield for the good will also serve as a sword for the
bad. This is as true of the First Amendment as it is of the Fifth.
No one has devised a rule that would protect Martin Luther King
Jr. without also protecting David Duke, or that would shield
James Joyce without providing a sword to Larry Flint. The law,
and especially the Bill of Rights, is not a scalpel; it is a blunt
instrument. It either protects too much or too little.

But Friendly fully understood this. Indeed, he repeatedly acted on it as a judge. He was among the most brilliantly result-
oriented judges, especially in criminal cases. When he believed a
defendant was guilty and deserving of punishment, he cleverly
distorted the record, ignored the law, misquoted counsel's argument, and did whatever he could to produce a "just" outcome.
When he had doubts about the guilt or culpability of the defendant, he would call it straight. This is all too common among
appellate judges, but Friendly was unusual in his openness about
what he thought to be the proper role of a judge's perception of
the defendant's probable guilt or innocence. The problem is that
appellate judges, including Friendly, rarely have the experience,
expertise, information, or mind-set by which to evaluate the underlying facts of a case or to assess the probable innocence or guilt
of a particular defendant.

Nor did Friendly have the requisite background to understand
how the "rules of law actually work" in criminal cases. His writing
about the privilege is filled with misunderstandings and mistakes
about how the privilege operates in practice. One of Friendly's

major complaints, for example, was that the privilege denies the government the power to elicit potentially incriminating information for uses other than to prosecute the defendant:

> The privilege, at least in its pre-trial application, seriously impedes the state in the most basic of all tasks, "to provide for the security of the individual and his property," not only as against the individual asserting the privilege but against others who it has reason to think were associated with him. The privilege not only stands in the way of convictions but often prevents restitution to the victim—of goods, of money, even of a kidnapped child.

But in practice, it is rather easy for the government to achieve these other goals: all it has to do is grant derivative use immunity to the suspect and compel him to disclose the information. Friendly sometimes seems to remember immunity and sometimes seems to neglect it. He neglects it when railing against the doctrine that the privilege protects a defendant from producing incriminating documents, when the act of production itself would be incriminating:

> I favor an amendment that would abolish the privilege with respect to chattels, notably including documents, in the possession of the defendant which are sought to be obtained by reasonable subpoena or other legal process.... The arguments that compulsory production involves an implicit testimonial disclosure, to wit, "the witness' assurance... that the articles produced are the ones demanded,"... reeks of the oil lamp. Yet it is only this assumed authentication that brings the case within the words of the amendment "to be a witness against himself." The prosecution wants the chattels, typically

documents; it will find its own ways for authenticating them.
The dilemma thus is not of self-accusation and perjury but of
self-accusation and refusal to respect a court's process. It takes
a heart much more hemophilic than mine to find cruelty in
this.

Judge Friendly was apparently unaware that this "problem" could
be—and has been—easily solved by granting the subpoenaed
person an "act of production immunity." Under this now common
form of limited immunity, the suspect is assured that the fact that
he produced the documents will not be used against him, but that
the *content* of the documents will. The government will have to
authenticate them without using the fact that the subpoenaed
person produced them, but as Friendly acknowledged, "it will
find its own ways for authenticating them." This is a nonproblem.
It was a nonproblem when Friendly wrote about it. It did not need
an amendment to the Bill of Rights to solve it. Friendly was
simply mistaken.

He was also mistaken when he proposed that "substitute
counsel should be enough when waiting for the accused's own
counsel would result in substantial delay." This was part of his
proposal to require all defendants to answer incriminating questions put to them in the presence of their lawyer or face comment
by the judge about their refusal. Could a "substitute counsel,"
unfamiliar with the case or the client and brought in as a stopgap,
"reflect" on this difficult choice on the spur of the moment? Even
a lawyer familiar with the situation would have great difficulty
advising his client on which horn of the dilemma to hang his
liberty or life, without a far deeper knowledge of the facts and law
than he is likely to have at that point in time. Friendly's utter lack
of experience as a criminal defense lawyer led him to this unre-
alistic proposal for a stopgap, emergency-appointed lawyer.

Much of what Friendly wrote in 1968 has proved to be wrong or irrelevant to today's Fifth Amendment. The one point he repeatedly emphasized that *is* currently relevant is that "the element of compulsion or involuntariness was always an ingredient of the right," and that the right includes "a prohibition of the use of physical or moral compulsion to extort communications" and that it should be interpreted "to stamp out the 'third degree'—an affront to human dignity and a source of unreliable confessions." Though Friendly did not, to my knowledge, ever consider the issue presented in *Martinez*—whether the Fifth Amendment applies to physical coercion or the "third degree" employed to obtain information not to be used in a criminal case—he would probably have agreed with the majority, despite his acknowledgment that a primary focus of the privilege should be on coercion.

Judge Friendly's critique of the privilege, unsound as it was in its particulars, had a significant impact on subsequent judicial construction. Because it was titled "The Fifth Amendment Tomorrow," and because today is Friendly's tomorrow, his critique provides a good starting point for a discussion of the privilege today. But before we consider the scope of the privilege in the preventive state, one important contemporary critic must be addressed.

In 1997, Yale law professor Akhil R. Amar published a particularly cogent assessment of the self-incrimination clause. Amar's emphasis on truth and reliability—and his de-emphasis on more symbolic and abstract concerns, such as "cruel trilemma" and "parity"—lead him to reinterpret the Fifth Amendment consistent with what he believes its object should be: to improve the accuracy of the criminal justice system "by bringing more information into the system." This is certainly a commendable goal, but the means by which Amar seeks to achieve it raise important questions under the law of unintended consequences. He would apply the privilege's exclusionary remedy only to the coerced *testimony* itself, but not to its *fruits*. Because the fruits of a coerced confession—for example, the body that the confession led investigators to find—are generally self-proving, no reliability issues are raised by their admission. This "clean reading" of the privilege, according to Amar, is the most faithful both to the text of the Fifth Amendment and to its "big idea."

Amar would also empower the government to compel the defendant to testify about his involvement in suspected crimes at a pretrial deposition (as well as at other formal legal proceedings other than his own criminal trial). "The penalty for refusing to answer would be contempt, and the penalty for lying would be perjury." The compelled self-incriminating testimony would be excluded from the defendant's criminal trial, but "virtually all physical evidence and third party testimony that the defendant's statements led to would be admissible." Amar believes that this orderly process for compelling incriminating information—orderly in the sense that the defendant would have a lawyer and the proceeding would be presided over by a judge—would essentially *replace* today's station-house interrogation. Here is his argument in a nutshell:

> [A] civilized process would exist outside the police station to compel suspects to talk truthfully, and so the police would be less tempted to force the issue. In light of this civilized alternative, courts might well choose to police the police even more strictly than today, enforcing a prophylactic rule that no police station confession by a defendant is ever allowed in unless volunteered by a suspect in the presence of an on-duty defense lawyer or ombudsman, or unless the defendant consents to its introduction at trial. Rooted in a legitimate concern about unsupervised police compulsion, this strict regime

would create powerful incentives to conduct interrogation before magistrates rather than in police stations.

Amar does not tell us how his scheme would deal with the *fruits* of a station-house confession coerced by police misconduct. And that is the key to whether the "police would be less tempted to force the issue" and whether his "regime would create powerful incentives to conduct interrogations before magistrates rather than in police stations." Every police officer understands the enormous difference between a station-house interrogation of an unrepresented, unprepared, and frightened suspect, on the one hand, and the formal questioning of a "lawyered-up," well-prepared defendant, on the other hand. In the eyes of the police, the latter is no substitute for the former. Cops want to solve crimes in real time. They want to find the body while it is still warm—or even better, still alive. They understand that confessions offered under the pressure of police interrogation may be faulty, but the physical evidence to which they may lead will often be self-proving and crime solving.

Antiterrorism investigators want real-time intelligence. They care less about whether "confessions" can be admitted into evidence at a criminal trial than about stopping terrorist attacks. Police and investigators will thus have considerable incentives to continue to interrogate vulnerable suspects, especially if they can still use the fruits of such interrogation to do *their* crime-solving and prevention jobs, which are considerably different from the job of the prosecutor to convict the defendant at a criminal trial.

Amar's elegant solution is therefore unlikely to eliminate, or even reduce, the practice of station-house interrogation, or, in his words, to "curb the temptation to police abuse." It is likely, however, to increase the amount of defendant perjury and to exacerbate the ethical problems of defense lawyers in preparing their client to provide the compelled testimony in front of a judge. (More about this later.) Nor is Amar's "clean reading" of the Fifth Amendment as clean as he suggests. The privilege prohibits the government from compelling any person to be a witness against himself in any criminal *case*. It takes something of a textual sleight of hand to regard the pretrial deposition of a criminal suspect as not part of his criminal case. Had the framers used the word "trial" instead of "case," the textual argument might be more persuasive. But "case" is broader and more inclusive than "trial." When I consult on a pretrial criminal investigation, as I often do, I am working on my client's "case," though not on his trial. If I am successful, there will never be a trial. The *case* will end with a declination to prosecute and a decision to forgo a *trial*.

This textual point may sound rather technical, but it should be significant to Amar, for whom the choice of words by the framers is crucial. He rightly points out that the framers used the word "witness" in the Fifth Amendment rather than the more inclusive word "evidence" that some state constitutions had employed. This is how Amar develops that argument:

> Only the defendant's compelled testimony should be protected by the amendment. The "witnessing" that the defendant has a right to exclude from the criminal trial includes both statements on the stand at trial and the introduction at trial of any earlier compelled depositions. This definition of witness closely tracks what seems to be the best definition of witness under the confrontation and compulsory process clauses of the Sixth Amendment. Unlike some state constitutions, such as the Massachusetts Constitution of 1780, the Fifth Amendment does not prohibit the government from compelling a defendant to furnish evidence against himself. Compelled fruit is admissible, but compelled testimony is not.

But Amar begs a similar question with regard to the word "case," as distinguished from "trial":

> Textually, the Fifth Amendment speaks to *witnessing* within the criminal case, not beyond. Therefore, the key question is what "witnessing" is excludable "in" a "criminal case"—that is, at trial.

But the phrase "that is" cannot transmogrify the word "case" to the very different word "trial." In a somewhat tortured footnote, Amar argues that "pre-trial proceedings" should not be included within a self-incrimination clause "case," but his argument is more of a brilliant advocate's brief than a historian's clear-eyed assessment.

Finally, Amar's proposal does not address the issue raised in *Martinez* or the more general issue of whether the government can constitutionally use rough interrogation tactics and even torture (or torture-like methods) to elicit *preventive* information not intended to be used in a criminal trial. Amar acknowledges that the "founding-era history of the self-incrimination slogan in America was bound up with concerns about torture." He argues, however, that "the root anti-torture idea is largely a Fourth Amendment idea and not a Fifth Amendment idea." He claims that this is "prove[d]" by the fact that "even criminal witnesses and civil witnesses and parties—and everyone else, too—must be protected against torture."

But that does not prove Amar's conclusion. Remember that the framers used the broad term "no person" in the Fifth Amendment rather than the narrower term "the accused" that they used in the Sixth Amendment. They used similar terms—"the people" and "secure in their persons"—in the Fourth Amendment. What little discussion there was of torture in the context of enacting the Bill of

Rights occurred with reference to the Fifth, not the Fourth Amendment. This "legislative history" and choice of language not only fails to prove Amar's point; it suggests that the Fifth Amendment was intended not only as an exclusionary rule for criminal cases, but also as a more general prohibition on the use of torture and other impermissible forms of compulsion against *all* persons. But this plausible reading does not fit neatly into Amar's "holistic constitutional account," so he rejects it in favor of one that does.

Moreover, even Amar's "holistic" account does not always point in one direction. The right against self-incrimination was specifically included among the Fifth Amendment rights of which "no *person*" could be denied, rather than among the Sixth Amendment rights to which only "the *accused*" was entitled. This placement, viewed holistically, would seem to support a general right applicable beyond criminal cases to all persons, whether or not accused of a crime. But then, at the last minute, this structurally neat placement was disturbed by a hastily proposed word change that added "in any criminal case" to an amendment that applies to all persons.

Had the proponent of the word change suggested that the right against self-incrimination be eliminated from the Fifth Amendment and added to the Sixth Amendment, he might have generated a substantive debate about the intended scope of the right. But instead he apparently viewed it as a technical change designed to address a specific issue then pending in Congress and in the New York courts. How, then, would a holistic approach deal with this nonholistic change in the scope of the right against self-incrimination? Amar's construct provides no answer to this question. I have nothing but praise, expressed more gratefully elsewhere, for Amar's heroic efforts to construct a holistic architecture of the Constitution. But we must remember that it is a *construct*

[149]

rather than an always faithful effort to discern the original understanding of this pragmatic document that never had a singular original understanding.

No one can know what each of the framers (and those who ratified the Bill of Rights) understood by the delphic, contradictory, confusing, misunderstood, anachronistic words—some, such as "in any criminal case," inserted at the last minute with little discussion or explanation. All we can know is that they feared governmental abuse such as torture, the oath *ex officio*, and some other forms of compelled self-incrimination, and that they sought to constitutionalize these concerns in an enduring document designed to protect the liberty not only of their contemporaries but of future generations in changing time and circumstances.

Amar's useful construct lies somewhere between an attempt to discern the understanding of the framing generation and an effort to reconcile the broad policies underlying the Constitution as a whole. In his own words, his work is designed to "show" how it all "fits together." The problem is that it doesn't always fit together, at least not without the sort of intellectual shoehorn Amar employs. Sometimes the foot fits snugly into the shoe. Sometimes it has to be forced. Other times, it simply doesn't fit.

Constitutional law scholarship, in general, suffers (or perhaps benefits) from the multiple functions it seeks to serve: historical, interpretive, constructive, functional, heuristic, ideological, adversarial, among others. The "is" (or "was") is often conflated with the "ought." More precisely, the "is" (or "was") is distorted to serve the interests of the "ought." "Theories" of constitutional "law," "interpretation," "construction," "adjudication," and "analysis" are often attempts to construct a general approach out of ambiguous words, fragmentary evidence of past intentions, lost understandings, and anachronistic concerns.

As I have written previously about Ronald Dworkin in a related context: "[Dworkin] locates such non-positive rights within a 'constructive model,' which human beings build 'as if a sculptor set himself to carve the animal that best fits a pile of bones he happened to find together.'" Any effort to construct general theories of constitutional law, applicable to current issues but based on past understandings, will necessarily conflate the descriptive with the prescriptive. That is why it is important to distinguish the *policy* arguments for a vibrant right against self-incrimination, which I will now seek to present, from the purely *constitutional* arguments for such a right.

POLICIES UNDERLYING THE PRIVILEGE
AGAINST SELF-INCRIMINATION

The policy arguments for and against the privilege fall into several distinct categories: constitutional (previously discussed), civil libertarian, moral, and political. All of these overlap, but also raise somewhat distinctive questions.

To assess competing policy considerations, the privilege must be deconstructed functionally. First, there is the supposed right to remain silent. This raises questions of what such a right would entail and whether it could ever be anything more than symbolic. Second, what constraints should be placed on governmental efforts to elicit information that may be self-incriminating but that may also be important to achieving goals other than prosecuting the person being interrogated? Third, there is the question of remedies, namely, whether violations of the privilege should be subject to such remedies as injunction, criminal punishment, and civil liability, or whether the sole remedy should be exclusion of the evidence from a criminal trial. Fourth, there is the issue of immunity and its functional analogues. Is derivative use immunity really coterminous with the privilege? Are there valid analogies between immunity and improper means of interrogation?

Underlying all these issues are the broad questions—raised by Friendly, Amar, and others—of whether the privilege, narrowly or broadly defined, can be justified, whether it has become anachronistic, whether there is any historical basis for its current scope, and whether there might be better ways to achieve the goals of the privilege than by its current formulation and interpretation.

I shall briefly explore each of these issues in turn. To assess the current utility of the privilege, and balance it against its obvious costs, it will be useful to imagine a criminal justice system without the privilege. It will also be useful to deconstruct the privilege into its several components and to assess each of them separately. In the end, it may turn out that one or more of the components is more (or less) justified than others.

THE DEFENDANT'S PRIVILEGE

Let us begin with the "defendant's privilege," which is directly mandated by the text of the Fifth Amendment. It prohibits the prosecution from calling the defendant as a witness at his own criminal trial. When evaluated in the context of the criminal justice system at the time of the framing, the defendant's privilege seems unnecessary, at least if interpreted literally. Even absent the privilege, prosecutors could not call a defendant as a "witness" at his own criminal trial because criminal defendants were disqualified from testifying under oath at their own trials, even if they wanted to do so. The defendant was allowed to *speak* in his own defense, but only as an *unsworn* advocate. Most defendants did not have lawyers, and the only person who could speak for them was themselves. If they chose not to speak, they would be presumed guilty, especially because there was no instruction advising the jury not to infer guilt from the defendant's silence.

Over time, the defendant's right not to be called as a witness by the prosecution has evolved into an important right that profoundly affects current trials. It is accompanied by a constitutionally required instruction informing the jury that it may not infer guilt from the defendant's exercise of that right, and also by an instruction placing a heavy burden of proof on the prosecution in order to overcome the defendant's presumption of innocence. All defendants facing serious charges have a constitutional right to be provided a lawyer if they cannot afford one.

The vast majority of defendants today plead guilty, but among those who go to trial, most exercise both their right to be represented by counsel and their right to remain silent. The vast majority of those defendants who go to trial are convicted, regardless of whether they testify or remain silent. Defendants who exercise their right to remain silent are probably more likely to be convicted than those who choose to testify. But if this is so, it is probably because defendants without criminal records are more likely to testify than defendants with prior convictions, and that defendants with criminal records are more likely to be (or to seem) guilty than defendants without criminal records. It is also likely that innocent defendants are more willing to undergo cross-examination, and it is certainly possible that despite the jury instruction, many jurors do take a defendant's silence into account in evaluating guilt or innocence.

As a practical matter, the entire trial dynamic changes when a defendant takes the stand. Weaknesses in the prosecution's case tend to be overshadowed by the jury's focus on the defendant's credibility, demeanor, and responsiveness. Criminal defense lawyers disagree about the risks and benefits of exposing defendants to cross-examination, but it is certainly a crucial decision.

It is far from clear whether the defendant's privilege has any real impact on the *accuracy* of criminal trial verdicts, and if it does, whether it produces more false acquittals or false convictions. It is clear, however, that it reduces the amount of perjury at criminal trials. A silent defendant is a nonperjuring defendant. A testifying defendant, if he is guilty, is likely to perjure himself. (Even if he is innocent, a defendant might perjure himself.)

On the other hand, as I have written elsewhere, far more perjury is today committed by prosecution witnesses than by defense witnesses (and even more by civil litigants). This is not because defendants or their witnesses are more honest than prosecutorial witnesses (or civil litigants), but because prosecutors (and civil litigants) *must* put on witnesses, including "testalying" police officers, "bought," "rented," and "flipped" accomplices, and other assorted associates of the accused, whereas the defense need not put on any witnesses, and in many trials limits itself to cross-examining the government's witnesses. Whoever presents witnesses will, with some frequency, put on lying or perjuring witnesses. Because criminal defendants generally do not testify, they generally do not commit perjury. This would all change if defendants were required to testify.

The dynamics of the trial would change in other ways as well. In some cases, the prosecutor would call the defendant as a hostile witness expecting him to commit perjury. In other cases, the defense would call the defendant, fearful that failure to do so would create a presumption of guilt. If the defense attorney calls the defendant as a witness, he must "vouch" for his truthfulness; he cannot ethically call him if he knows he will testify falsely. This is even more complex in a criminal than in a civil trial, because a criminal defendant has a constitutional right to testify (as well as not to testify). Defendants sometimes insist on testifying despite their lawyer's advice to the contrary. Under current rules, if the defense attorney does not call the defendant to the stand, it is a red flag signifying that the lawyer may know that his client would commit perjury. The abolition of the defendant's privilege would fundamentally change the dynamic of the lawyer-client privilege, discouraging (even more than today) defendants from disclosing their guilt to their attorneys.

The defendant's privilege, on balance, does less harm to the process than would its abolition or significant narrowing. It ain't broke, and there is no good reason to fix it. Although it serves quite different purposes than it did at the time of the framing, it fits comfortably (if accidentally) into our current system of criminal justice. Its abrogation would violate the law of unintended consequences. It would also tamper with an important balancing mechanism in our existing adversary system without a compelling reason.

THE WITNESS'S PRIVILEGE

The second component of the privilege that warrants reconsideration is the witness's privilege. It permits a sworn witness in any legal proceeding to refuse to answer specific questions on the ground that a truthful answer might tend to incriminate him. The witness's privilege does not derive directly from the text of the Fifth Amendment. Nor does it flow inexorably from the language or policies of the defendant's privilege. It must stand or fall on its own merits and on its historical lineage.

Unlike the defendant's privilege, which is absolute and has no mechanism for circumvention, the witness's privilege is easily overcome by a grant of derivative use immunity, which is supposed to put the witness in precisely the same situation he would have been in had he invoked the privilege. When immunity is granted, the government, at least according to the theory of immunity, loses no information. Nor does it, in theory, diminish its prospects for securing a criminal conviction. It may use any evidence independently discovered and not derived from the information obtained from the defendant after he has been granted immunity.

In reality, neither the government nor the defendant is really in the same position. The government must satisfy a heavy burden of demonstrating an independent source, and the witness has been compelled to reveal embarrassing, damaging, and even bankrupting information. The defendant who has been compelled to testify under a grant of derivative use immunity also sometimes constrains the tactical and ethical options available to his counsel at trial. But the core policies of the privilege have been served. This still leaves open the question whether the benefits of the witness's privilege are worth the costs, even if the costs are relatively minimal.

In at least one context the cost of the witness's privilege clearly exceeds its benefits: when the defendant in a criminal case seeks exculpatory evidence from an alleged accomplice who is cooperating with the government. Only the government has the statutory power to immunize the witness, and in such circumstances it almost never does so, even if it has no intention of prosecuting the witness. It refuses immunity purely on self-serving, tactical grounds: namely, that the witness's testimony might benefit the defendant. Moreover, prosecutors in this situation often encourage the witness to invoke his privilege—and because they have extraordinary leverage over cooperating witnesses, this "encouragement" often translates into compulsion. Some courts have held that in extreme situations the Sixth Amendment may require the government to grant "defense immunity" to an exculpatory defense witness, but such extreme situations rarely arise.

A literal interpretation of the Fifth and Sixth Amendments should lead to the conclusion that the criminal defendant's textual right under the Sixth amendment—"in all criminal prosecutions, the accused shall enjoy the right . . . to have compulsory process for obtaining witnesses in his favor"—must trump the privilege of the witness whose testimony the defendant seeks, since the witness's privilege is not mandated by the text of the Fifth Amendment. Because derivative use immunity is supposed to put *both* sides in the position they would have been in had the witness's privilege been exercised, it is difficult to justify the government's refusal to grant immunity when the defendant can make a plausible showing of need for the testimony of the witness. This is one context in which current case law clearly should be modified in the interests of fairness and of the Sixth Amendment.

Some courts have argued that they are not empowered to grant immunity because that decision must be made by the executive branch, and for a court to preclude prosecution would violate the separation of powers. This argument might have force if transactional immunity were required—that is, immunity that would preclude prosecution altogether. But all that is required here is derivative use immunity, and such immunity—at least in theory— places the prosecution in the same position it would have been in without immunity. Such immunity has, in fact, been mandated by the courts as a matter of constitutional law in other contexts, even in the absence of legislative authorization.

The Supreme Court ruled in *Murphy v. Waterfront Commission* that states, cities, interstate agencies, and other units of government can impose derivative use immunity on federal prosecutors. It would seem to follow that a federal judge—in the interest of protecting a defendant's Sixth Amendment rights—should be able to impose that same kind of immunity on federal prosecutors. The separation of powers argument cannot trump a defendant's valid claim, any more than a federalism argument can. Accordingly, whenever a criminal defendant can make a plausible showing that his defense might benefit from the testimony of a witness who asserts the privilege, the judge should compel the witness to answer. The government, which has long argued that derivative use immunity places both parties in the same position when it grants such immunity in order to compel testimony to bolster the government's case, should not be heard to claim that it is unfairly disadvantaged by a similar grant of immunity that would help the *defense*.

Interestingly, the force of the defense immunity argument has been strengthened by the Court's analysis of the privilege in *Martinez*. If a witness has no primary right to remain silent, but only a remedial right to exclude compelled self-incriminating statements and their fruits, and if the point of impact of the right is the criminal trial of the witness who has been compelled or coerced to make a self-incriminating statement, then it would seem to follow that a witness at *another* person's criminal trial has no right not to testify. His *only* right after *Martinez* is the right to exclude compelled self-incriminating statements and their fruits from his *own* criminal trial, if he is ever prosecuted. That remedy is preserved by the derivative use immunity he would automatically secure by being compelled to answer self-incriminating questions.

Moreover, even if a witness has a right not to testify, that right should be subordinate to the defendant's Sixth Amendment right to obtain witness in his defense. This should be an easy issue. It is made to seem difficult only because of the predisposition of judges (many more of whom were former prosecutors than former defense attorneys) to see the issue from the adversarial perspective of prosecutors. Akhil Amar, who generally seeks to narrow the Fifth Amendment, agrees that a defendant's Sixth Amendment right "to have compulsory process for obtaining witnesses in his favor" should trump a witness's right against self-incrimination.

Apart from this issue—which unfairly advantages the government and disadvantages the defendant, and which can easily be remedied by judicial or legislative action—the witness's privilege, as currently understood, causes no serious problems. The government loses an occasional case because of the witness's privilege, as it did in the famous Oliver North prosecution, but in general the government can control its potential losses by making wise cost-benefit assessments about when to grant immunity to a witness. Problems may arise in the context of legislative decisions to immunize a potential criminal defendant—as occurred in the *North* case—but these separation of powers problems, like the federalism problems, are inherent in our constitutional architecture. There is no reason to amend the Constitution or to appreciably change the witness's right against self-incrimination. With the one exception of the defendant's right to call a witness who invokes the privilege, this facet of the privilege is not broken.

THE SUSPECT'S PRIVILEGE

The third component of the privilege, and perhaps its most controversial, is what I call the "suspect's privilege" and what history refers to as the "confession rule." This component arguably has the weakest textual and originalist claims to constitutional status. It presupposes physical, psychological, or other forms of police coercion against a suspect in a station house, in a police car, on the street—and now in detention and/or interrogation facilities. When the Fifth Amendment was enacted, however, there were no police (as we now know them), and no informal interrogation of the kind made famous by such shows as *NYPD Blue*, in which Officer Sipowicz browbeats guilty suspects into admitting their crimes, and no special interrogation facilities for suspected terrorists.

There was, of course, a long history of torture preceding the enactment of the Fifth Amendment, but it was judicial torture, authorized and supervised by the courts. Despite the absence of historical records, there must have been informal torture as well, outside of the legal system. Indeed, Blackstone referred to torture as a matter of "State" rather than as a matter of law. But the contemporary context that has generated the rules governing the suspect's privilege—most especially the *Miranda* rule—was unknown to the framers. It is not surprising, therefore, that at least one early twentieth-century Supreme Court decision, *Brown v. Mississippi* (1936), suggested that the entire issue of police coercion and torture is not governed by the privilege against self-incrimination, but by the more general concept of due process.

In evaluating the policies underlying the suspect's privilege, consider the following thought experiment, similar in some respects to the proposals offered by Judge Friendly and Professor Amar. First, imagine the following "reform" to our criminal justice system: All police interrogation of suspects is banned on the ground that such interrogation is inherently coercive and unfair. The fruits of any police interrogation are excluded from evidence. (This differs from Amar's proposal.) Instead, all suspects (against whom there is a certain threshold of incriminating evidence) are required to go before a judge with a lawyer present. If the suspect cannot afford a lawyer, one is appointed, with ample time to prepare for his role. (This differs from Friendly's proposal.) The entire proceeding is videotaped. The judge asks the suspect in a respectful voice to respond to a series of relevant, fairly framed questions, based on the available evidence. For example: "Sir, it has been alleged that on such and such a day in such and such a place you killed so and so. Witnesses such and such claim to have observed the killing. Are they telling the truth? Did you kill the alleged victim? If so why?" Or, "Sir, it is alleged that you know of plans by an associate to engage in an imminent act of terrorism. Please disclose what you know."

The lawyer is permitted to object to the form of the question, to its relevance, and so on. He is also permitted to confer with his client after each question is asked. The suspect is required to answer the questions truthfully. If he refuses to answer, he can be held in contempt and imprisoned until he answers, and his refusal can be made known to the jury, if he is ultimately brought to trial. If he answers falsely, he can be prosecuted for perjury. The resulting videotape will be shown to the jury, if there is a criminal trial. The fruits of the judicial interrogation will be admissible at the defendant's trial.

This heuristic is similar to the current process of questioning a witness after he has received immunity—with one important difference: the suspect in the thought experiment does not get the benefits of immunity. His answers and their fruits can be used against him. Under the text of the Fifth Amendment, this procedure would be unconstitutional, since the questioning of the suspect under oath would almost certainly be regarded as part of a "criminal case" in which a potential defendant is being "compelled" to be "a witness against himself."

But putting aside the constitutional privilege against self-incrimination, what would be the policy arguments for and against such a process? In what ways would it change our current system—for better or worse? Would it increase or decrease the overall accuracy of the criminal process? Would it increase or decrease the number of false negatives—that is, guilty people who are currently not convicted? Would it increase or decrease the number of false positives—that is, innocent people who are currently convicted? Would it increase or decrease perjury? Would it change the nature of investigations? Would it help prevent acts of terrorism? What other values would it impact? What unintended consequences might it produce?

Consider the following variation on this thought experiment. Instead of requiring the suspect to answer judicially posed questions, imagine a system in which a so-called truth serum is perfected to the point where it is 100 percent accurate and totally harmless and painless. What would be the policy considerations in favor of and against the use of such a serum in a pretrial proceeding and the admissibility of its fruits?

There are, of course, considerable differences between compelling a suspect to answer questions by threatening him with contempt, and forcing him to take a truth serum. In the former situation he retains the ability to exercise some choice, even though it is a choice with consequences. Even the proverbial "offer that can't be refused" can be refused, as evidenced by the people throughout history who chose torture and death over collaboration and confession. Responding to questions under the influence of a truth serum denies all choice. The bravest or most stubborn of suspects cannot refuse to answer, if the serum works. In this respect, it is more than *truth* serum, it is *compulsion* serum. Imagine for heuristic purposes another serum that does not compel the suspect *to answer*, but if he chooses to answer it denies him the option *of lying*. That would be truth serum or, more precisely, an antilying serum. Current positron emission tomography (PET) scan technology appears to be moving in this direction and may someday come close to providing a check against certain kinds of lies. It would not compel a suspect to answer, nor would it compel a suspect who did answer to do so truthfully, but it would accurately detect lies.

If the unfairness and coercion inherent in most police interrogations were truly to be eliminated—along with torture, bribery, lies, and the threat of physical abuse—what policy arguments would remain against compelling truthful answers to incriminating questions?

Recall that today police are allowed to employ trickery, lies, threats of certain kinds, promises, and other forms of deception and psychological manipulation in order to get suspects to waive their right to counsel and to admit their crimes. In practice, the interrogation room is often imbued with an atmosphere of violence and physical coercion. (Remember Sipowicz!) None of this would be permitted in the judicial model (lawfully compelled truthful answers to incriminating questions) or in the scientific model (truth serum).

By isolating the right to remain silent from the abuses of police interrogation, these heuristics force us to think about whether there should be a stand-alone right to remain silent, or merely a right not to be physically or psychologically coerced into making self-incriminating statements. The nature of the right also bears on the nature of the remedy or remedies for its violation. It also forces us to think about why the police today remain free to employ such questionable means of inducing waivers and confessions in the station house and on the street, while judges remain so constrained in eliciting waivers and confessions in the courtroom.

Some of these differences may grow out of the divergent histories of the three facets of the privilege, particularly the emphasis placed on the judicial oath by the originators of the privilege. Recall that at the time of the ratification of the Fifth Amendment, there were no police and hence no station-house interrogations. The abuses of that age were largely *judicial* abuses committed by magistrates and justices of the peace. The primary abuses were interrogation under oath and, to use Jefferson's phrase, "judicial torture." Today's abuses are committed largely by police, FBI agents, and military interrogators. Tomorrow's abuses may be committed by scientists and other experts at eliciting preventive intelligence. The challenge is to devise processes that strike an appropriate balance between the legitimate needs of government for different types of information and the legitimate policies underlying the privilege.

AN ANTIDISESTABLISHMENTARIAN DEFENSE
OF THE FIFTH AMENDMENT

When I was a kid, we were taught that the longest word in the English language was "antidisestablishmentarianism," but we were never told what it meant. Curiosity led me to look it up and discover that it referred to a group of British political figures who might not have favored, as an *original* matter, the establishment of the Anglican Church as the official (established) church of England, but who were opposed, as a matter of then *current* policy, to the disestablishment of that church. It was a subtle but important distinction: being against or uncertain about whether an action should have been taken years earlier, but now being against undoing that action years later.

Jefferson, who strongly favored disestablishing the Anglican Church in Virginia, took an antidisestablishmentarian position with regard to slavery: he wished that the institution of slavery had never been introduced to the American colonies and he generally opposed its spread to new areas, but he also opposed its immediate abolition in places where slavery had become part of accepted folkways. He feared that freeing the slaves and allowing them to live side by side with whites would result in a race war, with better armed and better trained whites slaughtering the former slaves, and many white deaths as well.

I am making an antidisestablishmentarian case for the preservation of the right against self-incrimination in the United States in the twenty-first century. Reasonable people might well have been opposed to, or uncertain about, the adoption of the right against self-incrimination—in at least some of its forms—as an original matter back in 1793. They could plausibly have argued that we would have been better off adopting an approach to criminal justice that did not accord criminal defendants, witnesses, or suspects the right to refuse to admit their guilt or to provide the government with evidence that might form a link in the chain of self-incrimination (or to disclose self-incriminating information that might help prevent terrorist attacks). But the framers believed differently, and for whatever reasons—historical, moral, religious, empirical—they established a system of criminal justice that required the prosecution to prove the defendant's guilt without requiring him to acknowledge it.

This system, as it developed over time, placed a heavy burden of proof—beyond a reasonable doubt—on the prosecution. It also adopted other rules, practices, and approaches that became part of what we call the adversarial system of criminal justice and that grew out of, or were related to, the right against self-incrimination. Many of these rules, practices, and approaches have not been adopted by nations that have rejected the right against self-incrimination, including nations that have eminently fair systems of criminal justice. Some of these differences flow inexorably from the right against self-incrimination itself—for example, the rule prohibiting prosecutors or judges from commenting on, or the jury from inferring guilt from, the defendant's decision not to testify. Other differences are less directly related to the right against self-incrimination but are part of the adversarial system to which the right is central. These include the presumption of innocence, the heavy burden of proof on the prosecution, the right to counsel at an early stage in the criminal process, and the criminalization and prosecution of false exculpatory statements made by defendants and suspects (a practice that is alien to many systems that do not have a right against self-incrimination).

This last point is worth underscoring. In the United States, a defendant or suspect has the right to remain silent in response to questions that seek incriminating answers, but if he elects to speak, he must speak truthfully at the risk of criminal prosecution.

He may not even utter an exculpatory "no" if the truthful answer would be "yes." In some continental countries, the defendant or suspect has no right to refuse to answer incriminating questions, but if he answers them falsely, he does not expose himself to criminal prosecution. He *must* answer, but he is not necessarily expected to answer *truthfully* (or under oath).

I recall vividly a conversation with Israel's chief prosecutor following the appellate reversal of the conviction of John Demjanuk, the Ukrainian death camp guard known as "Ivan the Terrible" for his brutal treatment of Jews. The Israeli government was reluctant to release a man they regarded as a genocidal killer. I suggested that he be tried for perjury, since his testimony at trial was contradicted by the alibi he presented on appeal, based on newly released Soviet documents. The prosecutor was incredulous at my suggestion. "We don't prosecute criminal defendants for lying at their trials," she insisted. In the United States, it would have been an open-and-shut perjury case.

It is this important difference that gives rise to the "cruel trilemma" faced by a defendant or suspect whose truthful answers might tend to incriminate him: if he refuses to answer, he can be imprisoned for contempt of court; if he answers truthfully, he can be convicted of the substantive crime; and if he answers falsely, he can be prosecuted and convicted of perjury.

The third horn of this trilemma does not exist in many of the systems that lack the right against self-incrimination. Accordingly, if we were now to eliminate that right, we would *not* be adopting the continental system. We would instead be adopting a hybrid system that would be much more onerous to the defendant or suspect than either the current U.S. or the continental system. We would also be adopting a system in which perjury (and related) prosecutions would play a much larger role than they currently do in either the U.S. or the continental system.

In this new hybrid system, as a *condition* of defending himself, a defendant would risk a perjury prosecution. This would be true not only for guilty defendants, but for any defendant, whether guilty or innocent. It would be true even for defendants who are *acquitted*, because the prosecution could subsequently bring a perjury prosecution based on new evidence or in the belief that a second (or third, or fourth) jury might be less favorable to the defendant.

This new system—in which the price of pleading not guilty would be a possible perjury prosecution—would effectively undercut the double jeopardy guarantee, extend the statute of limitations, and increase the amount of perjury in the American criminal justice system. Today, criminal defendants rarely commit perjury, for the simple reason that they rarely testify on their own behalf. If the privilege were eliminated, perjury by criminal defendants would become pervasive. The change would also place even more pressure on defendants to plead guilty, because the price of pleading not guilty—already high under current sentencing practices—would skyrocket. A criminal defendant today can plead not guilty without risking a perjury prosecution if he elects not to take the stand. But if pleading not guilty were to require the defendant to testify and assert his innocence under oath, the intermediate option would no longer be available.

This change would dramatically affect the role of the criminal defense lawyer, who in the United States is ethically and legally prohibited from knowingly allowing his client to testify falsely. Today an ethical criminal defense lawyer can usually persuade his client to assert his right against self-incrimination and thus avoid the dilemma of suborning perjury by knowingly eliciting false testimony from his client.

Although Akhil Amar does not directly address these problems, he has little sympathy for the guilty defendant faced with a "cruel trilemma" of his own making:

One frequently mentioned rationale for the privilege is the "psychological cruelty" of the so-called cruel trilemma.... But our justice system has no such scruples about compelling self-damaging answers from a civil litigant.... Nor does our system object to forcing people to testify in criminal cases against friends and family.... Today a mother may be forced, under penalty of contempt, to testify against her son and send him to the gallows. Thus, as a descriptive theory, the psychological cruelty argument simply does not hold water. To make matters worse, it benefits only guilty defendants: there is no trilemma if one is innocent and says so.

Nor, I suspect, would Amar be too worried about the ethical dilemma faced by the criminal lawyer. Just advise the "guilty" client to tell the truth, even if the truth will *not* set him free! But as any experienced criminal lawyer can attest, it is far more complex than that.

Disestablishing the constitutional right against self-incrimination, after more than two centuries of development and elaboration, could have cataclysmic consequences—some intended, others unintended—for our complex and uniquely American system of criminal justice. Whenever one important moving part is taken out of an interactive mechanism, it will inevitably affect other parts of the machine. The question, therefore, is not whether *as a matter of first principles* the continental system is "better" than ours. It is, rather, whether it would *now* be better to eliminate a central right upon which so much of our current system has been built over time.

BROADER TRENDS

The Supreme Court's rejection of the fundamental right of all persons to remain silent, or not to be coerced, in favor of a narrow trial right of only criminal defendants to exclude compelled testimony from their criminal trials is part of several larger trends. The first is a general narrowing of broad human rights to narrow trial rights: the presumption of innocence is now fairly established as merely an evidentiary trial right, rather than a presumption that cloaks all citizens in their relationship to government.

The courts have upheld pretrial detention laws that shift the presumption away from release to confinement between the time of arrest and conviction—or acquittal! The "logic" of these decisions is not necessarily limited to defendants who are awaiting trial. If criminal defendants who are thought to be dangerous can be preventively detained, why can't the government also detain nondefendants who might be thought to be equally or even more dangerous? This critical question is being played out in the context of suspected terrorists who cannot be charged with any crime.

The "cruel and unusual punishment" clause is now limited to postconviction sanctions, thus apparently permitting painful procedures calculated to elicit preventive intelligence.

The "due process" clause is seen by some justices as a mere procedural protection applicable primarily in the context of trials and other legal proceedings, rather than as an important substantive limitation on government actions.

Another, related, trend is to limit rights, even among criminal defendants, to the innocent, or at least the arguably innocent. The broadening of the harmless error rule, the narrowing of habeas corpus, the limitation of "reasonable expectations of privacy" in the Fourth Amendment context, and the return to Wigmore's crabbed concept of the privilege against self-incrimination all reflect this trend.

This trend raises even broader issues regarding the increasing marginalization of the Constitution with regard to policy debates, academic discourse, and legislative resolutions of important issues of criminal procedure. Over the past half century, the Constitution has dominated consideration of these issues. The arguments tended to be about the *constitutionality* of governmental actions rather than about their *desirability*. Because courts played such an active role in striking the balance between security and liberty, other institutions tended to defer, even to the point of abdicating their responsibilities. Legislators and executives rarely considered the constitutionality of their actions, all too frequently resorting to the argument that "if what we're doing is unconstitutional, the courts will stop us." If an action was held unconstitutional, that ended the debate, because it left no option other than constitutional amendment. But if an action was held to be constitutional, that too tended to end the debate. The operative assumption is that if a practice is not unconstitutional, it must be good public policy. The narrowing of constitutional rights by the Supreme Court in recent decades makes it increasingly important for other institutions to broaden the debate over sound public policy.

It is with this phenomenon in mind that I now turn to the policies supporting more vibrant constitutional constraints on the gathering of preventive intelligence information.

FILLING IN THE BLACK HOLE WITH LAW

There currently exists a gaping constitutional "black hole" with regard to the actions of the "preventive state." Our Constitution was designed with the "reactive state" in mind. Its protections, particularly those embodied in the privilege against self-incrimination, fit relatively well into a system in which evidence is gathered for use against criminal defendants at their own criminal trials. The Fifth Amendment's exclusionary rule is supposed to disincentivize interrogators from coercing confessions, because coerced confessions and their fruits cannot be used against the defendant. It is also supposed to keep out of evidence coerced statements that may be insufficiently reliable in a system based on the proposition that it is better for the guilty to go free than for the innocent to be convicted.

The traditional constitutional model of pretrial police work viewed arrest, search, detention, and interrogation as steps leading to trial. The reality, however, is that current police practices are increasingly preventive in nature, seeking to preempt threats rather than to gather evidence to punish and deter wrongdoers. The courts have distinguished, not always wisely, between criminal punishment and other sanctions, regardless of how punitive the sanction might feel to the one on whom it is imposed. This legal labeling game purports to derive its rules from the words of the Constitution and history of the common law. But whatever its source, it produces results that often make little functional sense. As I have written elsewhere about the civil-criminal labeling game:

> The court must determine whether certain procedural safe-guards, required by the Constitution in "all criminal prosecutions," apply to various proceedings.... The legislature enacts a statute that restricts the liberty of one player—variously called the defendant, patient, juvenile ward, deportee, et cetera. That player must then convince the court that the formal proceeding through which the state restricts his liberty is really a criminal prosecution. The state, on the other hand, must show that the proceeding is really civil....
>
> In the course of this game's long history, prosecutors have succeeded with the help of the court, and all too often, without the opposition of "defense" attorneys, in attaching the civil label to a wide range of proceedings including commitment of juveniles, sex psychopaths, the mentally ill, alcoholics, drug addicts and security risks. Likewise, sterilization, deportation,

and revocation of parole and probation proceedings are regarded as civil. By attaching this label, the state has successfully denied defendants almost every important safeguard required in criminal trials. Invocation of this talismanic word has erased a veritable bill of rights.

Another labeling game more recently played by the Supreme Court involves the distinction between regulatory and punitive sanctions, as well as between preventive and punitive sanctions. This is what Chief Justice William Rehnquist wrote in *United States v. Salerno* (1987) in ruling that the pretrial preventive detention in a maximum security jail of a Mafia boss was not criminal punishment:

> The mere fact that a person is detained does not inexorably lead to the conclusion that the government has imposed punishment.... To determine whether a restriction on liberty constitutes impermissible punishment or permissible regulation, we first look to legislative intent.... Unless Congress expressly intended to impose punitive restrictions, the punitive/regulatory distinction turns on "whether an alternative purpose to which [the restriction] may rationally be connected is assignable for it, and whether it appears excessive in relation to the alternative purpose assigned [to it]."

Having set out these relatively meaningless criteria, the Court then applied them in a wooden manner that has dangerous implications for other preventive mechanisms:

> The detention imposed by the Act falls on the regulatory side of the dichotomy. The legislative history of the Bail Reform Act clearly indicates that Congress did not formulate the pretrial

detention provisions as punishment for dangerous individuals.... Congress instead perceived pretrial detention as a potential solution to a pressing societal problem.... There is no
doubt that preventing danger to the community is a legitimate
regulatory goal.... We have repeatedly held that the Government's regulatory interest in community safety can, in appropriate circumstances, outweigh an individual's liberty interest.
For example, in times of war or insurrection, when society's
interest is at its peak, the Government may detain individuals
whom the Government believes to be dangerous.... Even
outside the exigencies of war, we have found that sufficiently
compelling governmental interests can justify detention of
dangerous persons.

This dichotomy between punishment, on the one hand, and "a
potential solution to a pressing societal problem," on the other, fails
to acknowledge the reality that punishment *is* often the solution to
pressing social problems and that such solutions are often punitive
in every sense of the word. Similarly, the purported dichotomy
between "punishment for dangerous individuals" and "preventing
danger to the community" fails to recognize the overlapping nature
of these related mechanisms of social control. In any event, these
labeling games merely lead to the result-oriented negative conclusion that the constitutional jurisprudence governing criminal
punishment is *not* applicable to preventive, preemptive, or other
"regulatory" mechanisms, even when the look, smell, and sound
are the same as criminal punishment. When it walks like a duck
and quacks like a duck...

The cases that rely on these false dichotomies generally fail
to articulate an alternative jurisprudence that should govern
preventive or preemptive sanctions. They simply conclude that
the constitutional protections required in criminal cases are not

applicable, and that some watered-down procedures should be applied in an ad hoc manner.

Because no meaningful jurisprudence of preemption or prevention has yet been constitutionalized, there exists broad flexibility to devise and articulate a coherent, consistent, and functional jurisprudence of anticipatory governmental actions. But neither the Court nor the academy has filled this important gap.

The current preventive model is quite different from the traditional model of evidence gathering in preparation for a criminal trial. This is especially so in the context of terrorism, where prevention assumes major significance. Those whose job it is to gather information—by means of interrogation, electronic intercepts, spying, and other low- and high-tech mechanisms—may have little or no interest in the admissibility of that information at subsequent criminal trials. Their interest is in real-time *actionable* information that can be used to prevent *future* crimes, especially terroristic ones. Exclusionary rules have even less impact on their actions than they do on traditional police actions in ordinary criminal investigations.

Pursuant to the Supreme Court's holding and reasoning in *Martinez*, the privilege against self-incrimination now has nothing to say about coercive interrogation, even that which entails torturous methods, so long as its fruits are not introduced into evidence at the criminal trial of the coerced person. The privilege, as interpreted by the Court, gives a green light to all preventive intelligence interrogation methods. The due process clause may impose some constraints on the most extreme forms of coercion, but even that is uncertain, especially in the context of preventing mass-casualty terrorist attacks.

The hole in our constitutional law is gray, if not black, when it comes to such interrogation. This is not as it should be in a nation that prides itself on the rule of law, especially constitutional law.

This gaping hole should be filled by meaningful constitutional safeguards. In Blackstone's England, a distinction could perhaps be drawn between "acts of state" and "acts of law," as Blackstone sought to do with regard to torture. But under our Constitution, all acts of State are governed by the rule of law. Our nation may not act except pursuant to the law and the Constitution.

If rights come from wrongs, as I have argued, then the right of all persons to be free of extreme coercive interrogation, especially those entailing torturous methods, should be assured under our Constitution. Perhaps the Constitution does not mandate *positive* rules for preventive interrogations, akin to those mandated for evidentiary interrogation under *Miranda*, but it must surely contain a *bottom-line* prohibition against the *worst* sorts of coercion, even in the preventive context.

The Supreme Court's decision in *Martinez* should not be the last word on this issue. More work needs to be done by courts, by legislatures, by academics and by the people themselves to protect all of us against accepting a society that routinely employs abusively coercive interrogations.

The disparity between what Americans reasonably *believe* is a broad, universal right to remain silent and the narrow, technical, conditional, and limited trial remedy a small number of criminal defendants *actually have* in practice, is far too great for a healthy democracy. Citizens should know their rights, and there should be a close, if imperfect, fit between the hortatory and the enforceable. To accomplish this closer fit, there will have to be compromise at both extremes: the hortatory should be cranked down, and the enforceable should be cranked up. The gap should be closed by making it plain that Americans do *not* have an absolute right to remain silent and by making equally clear that our government does not have the absolute power to use all manner of coercive interrogation, even for preventive purposes.

The privilege against self-incrimination should be construed to impose restrictions on at least *some* means of coercion, even if the resulting information is never used against a defendant at a criminal trial. Such a construction would give meaning to the word "compelled" as well as the words "criminal case," and would be more consistent with the spirit and history of the right and the wrongs it was designed to combat.

If the courts are unwilling to impose meaningful constitutional limitations on government coercion, then the people themselves must demand such limitations. This may seem naïve. But we would do well to remember that that is how we got a Bill of Rights in the first place.

I end this book with a challenge. We need to develop a jurisprudence for the emerging preventive state. This jurisprudence should contain both substantive and procedural rules governing *all* actions—"acts of state" as well as "acts of law"—taken by government officials to prevent harmful conduct, such as terrorism. Black holes in the law are anathema to democracy, accountability, human rights, and the rule of law. I urge citizens, legislators, judges, and scholars to take up this important agenda.

Notes

. . .

CHAPTER I

4 it seeks to guard.'" Leonard Levy, *Origins of the Fifth Amendment* (Chicago: Ivan R. Dee, 1999), 18–19, quoting *Counselman v. Hitchcock*, 142 U.S. 547 (1891).

6 idealists, or mushy liberals." Ibid.

6 and hitherto unknown privilege." Alan Dershowitz, "A Pragmatic Approach to the Effect of the 5th Amendment upon Administration of Justice," Political Science 34, Prof. Wilson (Brooklyn College, New York, 16 May 1958). From the Brooklyn College Archive.

6 unnatural right against self-incrimination. I do not believe in "natural" rights or "divine" rights. I believe that rights are human responses to human wrongs. See Alan Dershowitz, *Rights from Wrongs: A Secular Theory of the Origins of Rights* (New York: Basic Books, 2004), 230.

7 ...penalty...for such silence." *Malloy v. Hogan*, 378 U.S. 1 (1964), at 8.

7 may lead a private life.'" *Murphy v. Waterfront Commission of New York Harbor*, 378 U.S. 52 (1964), at 55.

7 gives the subject a moment's thought." *Brown v. Walker*, 161 U.S. 591 (1896), at 637 (Field, J., dissenting). See also Telford Taylor,

"The Constitutional Privilege against Self-Incrimination," *Annals of the American Academy of Political and Social Science* 300 (July 1955): 117.

7   **feeling of abhorrence in the community."** *Brown v. Walker* at 637.

7   **self-accusation, perjury or contempt..."** *Murphy v. Waterfront* at 55.

8   **offends due process."** *Culombe v. Connecticut,* 367 U.S. 568 (1961), at 602.

8   **either retained or appointed."** *Miranda v. Arizona,* 384 U.S. 436 (1966), at 444.

000   **making its assertion costly."** *Griffin v. California,* 380 U.S. 609 (1965), at 614.

8   **shoulder the entire load..."** *Murphy v. Waterfront* at 55.

000   **of our adversary system."** *Miranda v. Arizona* at 460. See *Griffin v. California*; *Lakeside v. Oregon,* 435 U.S. 333 (1978), at 336.

8   **only a few decades ago.'"** *Chavez v. Martinez,* 538 U.S. 760 (2003), at 783 (Scalia, J., concurring in part).

9   **securing an incriminating statement."** *Chavez v. Martinez* at 797 (Kennedy, J., concurring in part and dissenting in part).

9   ***Self-Incrimination* Clause occurs."** *Chavez v. Martinez* at 767.

9   **unwarned but voluntary statements."** *United States v. Patane,* 542 U.S. 630 (2004), at 633–34.

9   **[un-Mirandized] utterances."** *Harris v. New York,* 401 U.S. 222 (1971), at 226.

CHAPTER 2

12   **so long as the resulting "testimony"** Justice Souter apparently confuses "testimony" with "evidence." "Martinez's testimony" would not be at issue if it were the police who *testified* as to his unsworn earlier statements.

12   **justice accepted the view** The National Police Accountability Project and the National Black Police Association filed an amicus brief on behalf of the respondent, arguing that: "The Fifth and Fourteenth Amendments to the Constitution are violated when police officers coerce a statement from a suspect, regardless of whether this statement is ever introduced in a criminal trial, and regardless of whether there is a criminal trial" (2001 U.S. BRIEFS 1444).

14   **set out, somewhat antiseptically,** The majority justices certainly know how to write nonantiseptic opinions when it serves their interests to do so. See Paul Barrett, "There Is Blood on an Opinion, We Know Who Wrote It—The Supreme Court Justices (and Their Clerks) Stamp Prose with Quirky Flair," *Wall Street Journal,* 4 Oct. 1993, A1.

17   **O. M.: I think so.** The reason the police may have been interested in whether Martinez thought he was going to die is that there is an exception to the "hearsay rule" for statements made in contemplation of death.

19   **treatment for extreme pain.** "The 'enhanced interrogation techniques,' as the CIA calls them, include feigned drowning and *refusal of pain medication for injuries.* The tactics have been used to elicit intelligence from al Qaeda leaders such as Abu Zubaida and Khalid Sheik Mohammed." Dana Priest, "CIA Puts Harsh Tactics on Hold," *Washington Post,* 27 June 2004 (emphasis added).

20   **That remains to be seen.** For subsequent history of the case on remand, see Ninth Circuit No. 00-56520 at 10390; 542 U.S. 953 (2004); 229 F.R.D. 159 (2005), at 161; C.D. Cal. 23 June 2005, at 9; 9th Cir. Cal. 14 Aug. 2006; and 127 S. Ct. 1813, 2007.

20   **constraints on government.** See *United States v. Carlton,* 512 U.S. 26 (1994), at 40; *City of Chi. v. Morales,* 527 U.S. 41 (1999), at 85.

20   **violative of due process.** For the view that the *procedural-substantive* distinction is too sharp and that, in reality, *procedural* rules encompass *substantive* content, see Alan M. Dershowitz, "Preventive Confinement: A Suggested Framework for Constitutional Analysis," 51 *Texas Law Review* (1973), at 1295.

21   **to serve a "justifiable government interest."** Justice Thomas's criteria—that the coercive interrogation must intend to injure "in some way unjustifiable"—reminds me of a meeting I once had with a former Israeli pilot who had been captured by Syria and tortured for months before he was exchanged for Syrian prisoners. He told me that his torturer was now living in California. I offered to bring suit against him on the pilot's behalf, but he refused, saying, "He was a good soldier and he never tortured me more than was necessary." He then added, "And he didn't get any pleasure from it."

21   **due process or the privilege against self-incrimination.** Nor would torture constitute "cruel and unusual" punishment, since the Court

NOTE TO PAGE 22

has ruled that this prohibition applies only to punishment imposed after trial and with "'unnecessary and wanton' inflictions of pain...that are 'totally without penological justification.'" *Hope v. Pelzer*, 536 U.S. 730 (2002), at 737, citing *Rhodes v. Chapman*, 452 U.S. 337 (1981), at 346. The U.S. Court of Appeals for the Eleventh Circuit seems to have approved of torture as a way of securing information necessary to find a victim of kidnapping. In *Leon v. Wainwright* (734 F.2d 770, 1984), the Miami police choked a suspect "until he revealed where [the victim] was being held." A dissenting state court judge characterized the policemen's actions as "'rack and pinion' techniques," but the federal appellate court unanimously held that this was merely "a group of concerned officers acting in a reasonable manner to obtain information they needed in order to protect another individual from bodily harm or death." The dissent disagreed:

> For the first time in history, and the majority concedes as much, there is articulated a distinction between violent police conduct, the purpose of which is to gain information which might save a life, and such conduct employed for the purpose of obtaining evidence to be used in a court of law. The majority holds that where the illegal conduct is motivated by the first consideration no coercive taint will attach so as to render inadmissible evidence subsequently obtained for the purpose of securing a conviction. In essence, evidence of the whereabouts of a victim may be obtained using "rack and pinion" techniques if the officer on the scene determines the situation life-threatening, and after the information sought has been extracted the status is "deemed" as if the illegality had never occurred—an eerie proposition which should be rejected outright for all too obvious reasons. (*Leon v. Florida*, 410 So.2d 201 at 206, 1982)

22   **analyzing these claims."** Justice Thomas said, "Our views on the proper scope of the Fifth Amendment's Self-Incrimination Clause do not mean that police torture or other abuse that results in a confession is constitutionally permissible so long as the statements are not used at trial; it simply means that the Fourteenth Amendment's Due Process Clause, rather than the Fifth Amendment's Self-Incrimination Clause, would govern the inquiry in those cases and provide relief in appropriate circumstances." He then concluded that in this case the circumstances

were not appropriate to grant relief. (*Chavez v. Martinez*, 538 U.S. 760 (2003), at 773.) Yet, elsewhere in the opinion, he appears to contradict this view and suggest that the privilege, rather than due process, is the appropriate provision under which to analyze all coercive interrogations: "We also do not see how, in light of *Graham* v. *Connor*, 490 U.S. 386, 104 L. Ed. 2d 443, 109 S. Ct. 1865 (1989), Justice Kennedy can insist that 'the Self-Incrimination Clause is applicable at the time and place police use compulsion to extract a statement from a suspect' while at the same time maintaining that the use of 'torture or its equivalent in an attempt to induce a statement' violates the Due Process Clause. *Post*, at 155 L. Ed. 2d, at 1012. *Graham* foreclosed the use of substantive due process analysis in claims involving the use of excessive force in effecting an arrest and held that such claims are governed *solely* by the Fourth Amendment's prohibitions against 'unreasonable' seizures, because the Fourth Amendment provided the explicit source of constitutional protection against such conduct. 490 U.S., at 394–395, 104 L Ed 2d 443, 109 S Ct 1865. If, as Justice Kennedy believes, the Fifth Amendment's Self-Incrimination Clause governs coercive police interrogation even absent use of compelled statements in a criminal case, then *Graham* suggests that the Due Process Clause would not."

22   the 1952 case of *Rochin v. California*, 342 U.S. 165 (1952).

23   **permit of constitutional differentiation.** The *Rochin* case is no longer good due process law under the *Graham* principle. Indeed, in *County of Sacramento v. Lewis*, 523 U.S. 833 (1998), the Court said that a *Rochin*-type case would "today be treated under the Fourth Amendment," but added that it would have the "same result." The reason it would have the same result, however, is that a Fourth Amendment search would have to satisfy the criteria of not being "unreasonable," but unreasonableness alone might not satisfy the much more demanding "shocks the conscience" test of substantive due process.

23   **what is in his stomach.** The analogy is not persuasive. The Fifth Amendment, which applies to "the mind," provides an absolute prohibition against compelled self-incrimination, whereas the Fourth Amendment, which applies to the stomach, prohibits only certain types of searches (unreasonable ones and some without warrants).

23   **controversial from the very beginning.** Thomas Jefferson, in a letter written in 1801, made an interesting point about tests that in-

volve conscience. See Thomas Jefferson to Elijah Boardman, 3 July 1803, quoted in Alan Dershowitz, *Finding Jefferson* (New York: Wiley, 2007), 197 (Appendix A).

24 **th' ol' 'shocks-the-conscience' test."** *County of Sacramento v. Lewis*, 520 U.S. 833 (1998) at 861.

24 **based on alleged due process violations** See U.S. v. Lanier, 520 U.S 259 (1997). See also Linda Greenhouse, "Justices Broaden Immunity for Officers," *New York Times*, 23 Jan. 2008.

CHAPTER 3

25 **time in which it is used."** Quoted in Alan Dershowitz, *America Declares Independence* (Hoboken, NJ: Wiley, 2003), 4.

26 **"I always pay it extra."** Lewis Carroll, *The Annotated Alice* (New York: Norton, 2000), 213.

26 **must be interpreted as the framers** "The framers" can be taken to mean any number of individuals and groups of individuals. See William Anderson, "The Intention of the Framers: A Note on Constitutional Interpretation," 49 *American Political Science Review*, no. 2 (June 1955), at 341; Leonard Levy, *Origins of the Bill of Rights* (New Haven: Yale University Press, 1999), 186.

26 **"three strikes" statutes.** Adam Cohen has pointed out the irony of recent Supreme Court decisions limiting punitive damages against giant corporations while allowing unlimited prison terms against repeat minor offenders. See "The Supreme Court's Crusade: Fairness for the Powerful," *New York Times*, 26 Oct. 2006.

27 **to "evolve" differing interpretations** I use the term "evolve" because it is a word used by common law courts. It is, in fact, a poor metaphor because biological evolution is purposeless, random, and accidental, whereas common law development is guided by purposive human hands.

28 **"concise" and "generic."** *Bram v. United States*, 168 U.S. 532, 548 (1897), at 543.

28 **"resident aliens."** *United States v. Balsys*, 524 U.S. 666 (1998), at 671.

29 **Read literally, it prohibits the government** Literally, only the federal government. See *Brown v. Mississippi*, 297 U.S. 278 (1936). But, as we shall see, the Fourteenth Amendment has been interpreted to

apply some, though not all, provisions of the Bill of Rights to the states. In *Malloy v. Hogan* (1964) the Court held the privilege applicable to the states.

30 **derived from compelled self-incrimination,** See the Constitutions of Virginia (§8), Massachusetts (Article XII), New Hampshire (Article XV), Maryland (Article XXII), Connecticut (Article I, Declaration of Rights, §8), Delaware (Delaware Declaration of Rights, §15), North Carolina (*A Declaration of Rights*, VII), Pennsylvania (Article IX).

30 **"to be a witness against himself."** Indeed, a 1936 Supreme Court decision, rendered before the privilege had been applied to the states through the Fourteenth Amendment, read the clause literally as having no application to the admission into evidence of confessions coerced by the police prior to trial. In *Brown v. Mississippi*, the Court said that the self-incrimination clause of the Fifth Amendment is limited to "the processes *of justice* by which the accused may be called *as a witness* and required to *testify*." The Court went on to say that "compulsion by torture to extort a confession *is a different matter*." That "different matter" was to be decided under the "due process" clause, not the privilege against self-incrimination. (This view has not been followed, and *Brown* has been understood as applying the due process clause because the Fifth Amendment had not yet been held applicable to the states. I cite it here only to show that a prior Supreme Court decision, of which Justice Thomas was aware, read the text of the self-incrimination clause narrowly to apply only to in-court testimony by the defendant.)

31 **inconsistent with the text—at least sometimes.** Scalia reportedly said that Thomas "does not believe in *stare decisis*, period." Ken Foskett, *Judging Thomas: The Life and Times of Clarence Thomas* (New York: HarperCollins, 2004), 281–82. Jeffrey Toobin, in his book *The Nine* (New York: Doubleday, 2007), at 103, writes: "At an appearance at a New York synagogue in 2005, Scalia was asked to compare his own judicial philosophy with that of Thomas. 'I am an originalist,' Scalia said, 'but I am not a nut.'" See also *South Carolina v. Gathers*, 490 U.S. 805 (1989), at 825 (Scalia, A., dissenting).

31 **when its fruits are admitted at the criminal trial.** See Justice Kennedy's dissenting opinion in Chavez at 783.

32 **settled when the Amendment was adopted."** *Bram v. United States* at 543.

32   **the facts of each particular case"** *Bram v. United States,* 168 U.S. 532 (1897), at 549. The Court used the word "evolved" in the context of "the courts [having] left the rule to be evolved," but the framers understood that courts would be playing that role, especially with a rule so closely related to the criminal trial process.

32   **we could not understand him."** Ludwig Wittgenstein, *Philosophical Investigations: The German Text, with a Revised English Translation* (Oxford: Blackwell, 2002), 241.

33   **Judiciary Act of 1789. See Levy, Origins of the Bill of Rights,** 187–89.

34   **"in open court" will suffice.** The treason provision was placed in the body of the Constitution before the ratification of the Fifth Amendment. Accordingly, a narrow reading of Article III, Section 3, could have permitted—as a matter of constitutional, as distinguished from evidentiary or common, law—a compelled confession in treason cases. This is one situation in which the right against self-incrimination, narrowly read, could have had some impact at the time it was enacted.

35   **in the absence of the Fifth Amendment.** It is possible, of course, that the relevant provisions of the Fifth Amendment were intended merely to constitutionalize an existing evidentiary rule, but that is exceedingly unlikely, since the rule prohibiting a defendant from being a witness at his criminal trial was far more than a mere rule of evidence: it was a central part of the entire system of criminal justice that nobody dreamed of changing. There would simply be no need to include part, though not all, of that systemic constraint in a provision of the Bill of Rights. More likely, the words selected for inclusion in the Fifth Amendment were imprecise and, as an earlier Supreme Court opinion put it, "generic" and "concise."

35   **Why twenty and not ten or fifty?** See Alan Dershowitz, *Genesis of Justice* (New York: Warner Books, 2000), 69.

36   **cannot leave it at that!** There is, of course, the related action of a musician interpreting the written notes of a composer. I recall a conversation with the great cellist Yo-Yo Ma, who is my neighbor, about his relationship to the music of Brahms. I said that he had played Brahms probably more often than Brahms ever heard his own music and asked him whether he had ever been tempted to improve upon Brahms by changing a note here and there. He was shocked by my suggestion. "Musicians interpret," he insisted, "we do not edit." He then added, "except when we improvise."

36 **of their barbarous ancestors.** Quoted in Sanford Levinson, *Our Democratic Constitution* (Oxford: Oxford University Press, 2006), ix.

37 **can be discovered by historical research.** See Akhil R. Amar, *America's Constitution* (New York: Random House, 2005), 320–21.

38 **those respected principles.** *Chavez v. Martinez* at 793–94.

CHAPTER 4

41 **or someone else's criminal trial.** The person being compelled might be required to raise an objection at the time of the compulsion in order to preserve the issue for trial, or to make it clear that he did not volunteer the information. But that is a separate issue from the constitutional requirement of a statutory grant of immunity.

41 **requiring an incriminatory answer."** *Kastigar v. United States*, 406 U.S. 441 (1972), at 461 (emphasis added).

41 **the privilege on 'compulsion' or 'use,' "** *Murphy v. Waterfront* at 57, n6.

42 **I drafted that footnote.)** *Murphy* does lend support to the argument that—in the context of federalism—there may be no requirement of an immunity *statute* to compel self-incrimination. All that may be required is that the witness be told authoritatively by the judge, *before* he is compelled to answer, that either the Constitution or a statute guarantees him derivative use immunity. As we shall soon see, in the context of a unitary system—where the compulsion and use both take place within the federal (or presumably a single-state system)—a more formal grant of immunity may be required.

42 **evidence that might be so used."** *Kastigar v. United States* at 445 (notes omitted).

43 **uninterrupted line of cases.** The Court reaffirmed the *Kastigar* rule in *United States v. Balsys*.

43 **not any primary right to remain silent?** Would such a witness have no legal remedy at the time he was compelled? Would he have to go to jail until he answered the self-incriminating questions? Would he have no right to remain silent absent a grant of derivative use immunity? Would he have to answer the incriminating question and then raise his right only at his subsequent criminal trial? Would the judge be acting properly by compelling the incriminating answer and leaving it to a

subsequent judge to rule on whether admission of the compelled answer (and its fruits) would violate the witness's right?

This may sound like a hypothetical situation since many jurisdictions have statutory provisions requiring a formal grant of immunity before a witness can be compelled to answer incriminating questions. But I experienced a real situation, several years ago, in which some members of Congress took the position that a congressional committee had the power to compel a witness to answer incriminating questions absent any grant of immunity. They sought to justify this position on the ground of separation of power: Congress had the power to compel testimony, and the courts had the power to enforce the right against self-incrimination only by excluding the testimony (and its fruits) from a subsequent criminal trial. (One can imagine the executive seeking to trump this separation of power argument by making one of its own: Congress has no power to interfere with a criminal prosecution by unilaterally denying the executive the use of evidence needed to prosecute. Congress, of course, does this all the time by legislating immunity statutes, but at least such legislation requires the approval of the executive, generally.) Eventually, the congressmen backed off their position and acknowledged that the case law supported the right of a witness to refuse to answer incriminating questions put to him at a congressional hearing absent a formal grant of immunity.

44 **applicable then and there.** Justice Kennedy raised this issue during the oral argument, asking the lawyer for the policeman the following question:

> Well, suppose in a civil case, the judge orders the witness confined to custody until he testifies in violation of what we can say in common parlance is his Fifth Amendment right to self-incrimination. Is that not a violation then and there to—to confine the—the defendant until he testifies?

In his answer, the lawyer said the following:

> I suggest, Justice Kennedy, that the result—that the holding in *Murphy against the Waterfront Commission* is inexplicable if you believe, as the Ninth Circuit does, that it is sufficient simply

to coerce an otherwise incriminating statement because in Murphy against the Waterfront Commission, *the holding of that case is that the State court was correct in requiring the witness to testify even though there wasn't a statute that protected him against incrimination because the Fifth Amendment itself provides the fail-safe* that if you are coerced into giving an otherwise incriminating statement, it cannot be used against you.

In fact, the actual holding of *Murphy* was not quite as permissive. The Court ruled that "at the time they refused to answer" the incriminating questions put to them by the state, the witnesses "had a reasonable fear," based on the existing case law, "that the federal authorities might use the answers against them in connection with a federal prosecution." Accordingly, it reversed the contempt conviction and "afforded [the witnesses] an opportunity," in light of the newly announced rule granting them derivative use immunity, "to answer the questions." In other words, before a witness can be lawfully compelled to answer an incriminating question—or be held in contempt for refusing to do so—he must at the very least *know* that the answer cannot be used against him. This certainly suggests that there is a constitutional right to remain silent in the absence of a formal assurance of immunity.

45 **witness any less "compelled."** Justice Thomas must have meant to say "any less 'self-incriminating' " rather than "any less *compelled*." Surely immunity doesn't eliminate the *compulsion* element; it is, however, supposed to eliminate the self-incrimination element.

45 **Self-Incrimination Clause occurred here.** *Chavez v. Martinez* at 769–70 (citations omitted).

46 **without the ticking bomb.** See Alan Dershowitz, "Tortured Reasoning," in Sanford Levinson, ed., *Torture: A Collection* (Oxford: Oxford University Press, 2004), 257; Alan M. Dershowitz, "Is It Necessary to Apply 'Physical Pressure' to Terrorists—And to Lie about It?" 23 *Israel Law Review* 193 (1989); Alan M. Dershowitz, *Why Terrorism Works* (New Haven: Yale University Press, 2002), chap. 4; and Alan M. Dershowitz, "Is There a Torturous Road to Justice?" *Los Angeles Times*, 8 Nov. 2001, 19. Articles criticizing my approach: Jeremy Waldron, "Torture and Positive Law: Jurisprudence for the White House," 105 *Columbia Law Review* 1681 (Oct. 2005); David Luban, "Liberalism, Torture, and the Ticking Bomb,"

91 *Virginia Law Review*, no. 6, 1440 (Oct. 2005); Jonathan Sumption, "The New Machiavelli," *Spectator*, 29 Apr. 2006; Richard Posner, "The Best Offense," *New Republic*, 2 Sept. 2002, 28.

46 **in the ticking bomb situation.** Interestingly, former president Bill Clinton did agree with my proposal (see Alan Dershowitz, "Clinton and I," *New York Sun*, 18 Oct. 2006), but no Democratic presidential candidates, including Hillary Clinton, would support it. (See Peter Canellos, "Terrorism, Torture, and Shared Hypocrisy," *Boston Globe*, 9 Oct. 2007.)

47 **at least under the privilege.** If contempt is deemed criminal, then the prohibition of cruel and unusual punishment might come into play (in addition to due process), but civil contempt might not be categorized as punitive. See Dershowitz, "Preventive Confinement," 1295.

48 **at a coercion hearing is often risky.** In addition to the risk of perjury, there is the risk that the defendant may make statements that constrain further options.

49 **must be viewed with suspicion."** *Bush v. United States*, 375 F.2d 602 (1967), at 604.

49 **what all can see."** *People v. McMurty*, 64 Misc. 2d 63 (1970).

50 **derived from it become inadmissible.** *Kastigar v. United States* at 461–62 (notes omitted).

50 *Pillsbury Co. v. Conboy* 459 *U.S.* 248 (1983).

50 *United States v. Balsys.* 524 *U.S.* 666 (1998), at 683, *n*8.

51 **cuts both ways in the context of Martinez.** The dissent by Justice Thurgood Marshall in *Kastigar* also rejects the analogy between immunity and coerced confessions. See *Kastigar v. United States* at 470–71 (citations omitted) (Marshall, T., dissenting).

51 **analogies that may be artificial.** See, e.g., *Salerno v. United States*, 481 U.S. 739 (1987); *Schall v. Martin*, 467 U.S. 253 (1984) for an example of the Court falsely analogizing the pretrial detention of juveniles to the pretrial detention of hardened Mafia adult criminals.

CHAPTER 5

54 **worth a volume of logic.'"** *Ullmann v. U.S.*, 350 U.S. 422 (1956), at 438.

54 **judgments resting on other grounds."** Leonard Levy, "The Right against Self-Incrimination: History and Judicial History," *Political Science Quarterly* 84, no. 1 (Mar. 1969): 1.

55 **to interpret for Pharaoh."** *Youngstown Sheet & Tube Co. v. Sawyer*, 343 U.S. 579 (1952), at 634.

56 **as far as Europe is concerned."** Quoted in Waldron, "Torture and Positive Law," 1683–84.

59 **thoughtful men and women of the time."** R. H. Helmholz, "The Privilege and Common Law Criminal Procedure: The Sixteenth to the Eighteenth Centuries," in R. H. Helmholz et al., *The Privilege against Self-Incrimination: Its Origins and Developments* (Chicago: University of Chicago Press, 1997), 12.

60 **telling only a piece of it.** Quoted in Levy, *Origins of the Fifth Amendment*, at 42.

61 **ideological result orientation.** The phrase "activist judge" is thrown around by ideologues without any consideration of what the term "activist" actually means. Professor Paul Gewirtz and Chad Golder of Yale Law School ("So Who Are the Activists?" *New York Times*, 6 July 2005) sought to define that term by asking how often each justice has voted to strike down a law passed by Congress. They tabulated each justice's inclinations, regardless of whether he or she concurred with the majority or dissented: "Those justices often considered more 'liberal'—Justices Breyer, Ruth Bader Ginsburg, David Souter and John Paul Stevens—vote least frequently to overturn Congressional statutes, while those often labeled 'conservative' vote more frequently to do so. At least by this measure (others are possible, of course), the latter group is the most activist." See also Alan Dershowitz, *Supreme Injustice: How the High Court Hijacked Election 2000* (Oxford: Oxford University Press, 2001); Adam Cohen, "Last Term's Winner at the Supreme Court: Judicial Activism," *New York Times*, 9 July 2007, A16.

61 **Go to them that heard me."** Simcha Mandelbaum, "The Privilege against Self-Incrimination in Anglo-American and Jewish Law," 5 *American Journal of Comparative Law* 115 (winter 1956), at 119 (notes omitted).

62 **is a divine decree."** *Miranda v. Arizona* n. 27. See also Norman Lamm, "The 5th Amendment and Its Equivalent in the Halakah," 5 *Judaism* 53 (winter 1956).

62　cast themselves down from roofs." Quoted in Levy, *Origins of the Fifth Amendment*, at 438.

62　cutting one's own throat with one's tongue.") Levy, *Origins of the Fifth Amendment*, at 330.

63　Judgment was requested for money damages Jewish law permitted civil and criminal actions to be brought together in one proceeding.

63　violation of the rules of the Sabbath. Setting a fire on the Sabbath was considered by the Torah a criminal violation. Exodus 35 (3).

63　not for the purpose of criminal conviction. Maimonides, Mishneh Torah, Evidence, Ch. 12 (2) (1168).

63　to convict the witness for murder. Mandelbaum, "The Privilege against Self-Incrimination in Anglo-American and Jewish Law," at 118–19, citing T. Yebamot, 25b.

64　the rigors of the biblical requirements. These types of directive are called *takkanot*. They seek to "impose an obligation to act for the advancement of communal life and the promotion of the public welfare." See Menachem Elon, *Jewish Law: History, Sources, Principles* (Philadelphia: Jewish Publication Society, 1994), 491.

While Sanhedrin 6b stipulates that a person can be convicted only from the testimony of at least two witnesses, the rabbis would not allow a killer to go free after gathering "disjointed evidence" that pointed to the killer. Instead, they threw him in a cell and used a concoction of water and grain to cause his stomach to burst (Sanhedrin 81b). See www.come-and-hear.com/sanhedrin/sanhedrin_81.html#81b_19.

64　an act of "state" rather than "law." Sir William Blackstone, *Commentaries on the Laws of England*, vol. 4, 25, pp. 320–21, www.yale.edu/lawweb/avalon/blackstone/bk4ch25.htm.

65　earthly punishments, including death. In some respects this open-ended, general power to inquire under oath was similar to the dreaded general warrant that was later prohibited by the Fourth Amendment.

65　and scandal of many." Levy, *Origins of the Fifth Amendment*, 46, 47, 42, 271, 217, 49.

66　in relation to their king, The Great Writ took rights away from "the Jews": "If one who has borrowed from the Jews any sum, great or small, die before that loan be repaid, the debt shall not bear interest while the heir is under age.... And if anyone die indebted to the Jews, his wife shall have her dower and pay nothing of that debt."

67 **to be a witness against himself."** Leonard Levy, "Origins of the Fifth Amendment and Its Critics," 19 *Cardozo Law Review* (1997), at 837.

67 **linked to freedom of religion and speech.** Levy, *Origins of the Fifth Amendment*, 331.

68 **more important than punishing the guilty.** Levy, *Origins of the Fifth Amendment*, 383, 385, 405, 430, 430–31.

69 **"respond[ed] to the charges against him,"** John H. Langbein, "The Privilege and Common Law Criminal Procedure: The Sixteenth to the Eighteenth Centuries," in Helmholz et al., *The Privilege against Self-Incrimination*, 84, 89–90, 87, 95, 107, 108.

71 **the exercise of this right.** Defendant is entitled to an instruction to that effect if he requests one. Whether to request such an instruction—and highlight the defendant's refusal to testify—is a tactical decision.

71 **to present the defense case.** Theoretically, a defendant could represent himself, not testify, but make the opening and closing arguments. I participated, as a consultant, in one such case involving a political defendant.

71 **in his best interest not to testify.** Assume that a defendant confides in his lawyer that the only reason he does not want to testify is that he is afraid his testimony will hurt *his friend* or will reveal an embarrassing *but not criminal* act (say, adultery in a state where that is not criminal) or make a bad impression. It would be entirely appropriate for a criminal defendant to decide not to testify under these circumstances, and it would be entirely ethical for a lawyer to go along with that decision (so long as it did not compromise his ability to effectively represent his client—a somewhat more complex issue). The law is different with regard to the *witness's* privilege: a witness can refuse to answer *only* specific questions that could tend to incriminate him. If a lawyer asserted the witness privilege to protect a third person or to protect the witness from mere embarrassment, he would be acting improperly.

72 **some questioning must have been allowed** See Eben Moglen, "The Privilege in British North America," in Helmholz et al., *The Privilege against Self-Incrimination*, 114–17, specifically 117, which discusses the pretrial role of the justice of the peace.

73 **when an answer might incriminate him.** Levy, "Origins of the Fifth Amendment and Its Critics," 845–47.

73 **becoming self-confessed criminals.** Levy, *Origins of the Fifth Amendment,* 284, 231.

73 **answer truthfully under oath."** Levy, "Origins of the Fifth Amendment and Its Critics," 823.

73 **an essential part of the constitutional right.** With some exceptions, see *California v. Byers* 402 U.S. 424 (1971); *Jenkins v. Anderson* 447 U.S. 231 (1980).

73 **even without advice of counsel.** See Levy, "Origins of the Fifth Amendment and Its Critics," 842.

75 **he *must* take the stand.** In some situations, a judge will permit a witness not to take the stand if the judge knows that the witness will properly invoke the privilege as to all questions. (See trial of O. J. Simpson, in which police officer Mark Fuhrman was not required to plead the Fifth in the presence of the jury. Alan M. Dershowitz, *Reasonable Doubts: The O. J. Simpson Case and the Criminal Justice System* [New York: Simon & Schuster, 1996], 190.) This is highly questionable in light of the general rule that a fact finder can draw negative inferences from a *witness's* invocation of the privilege, but not from the *defendant's* in a criminal case.

76 **the authority of the subpoena or judicial compulsion** Some statutes now *require* a suspect to respond to certain limited police inquiries. See *California v. Byers*; *Hiibel v. Sixth Judicial Dist. Court,* 542 U.S. 177 (2004).

76 **somewhat different histories and policies.** Langbein, "The Privilege and Common Law Procedure: The Sixteenth to the Eighteenth Century," citing Henry E. Smith, "The Modern Privilege: Its Nineteenth-Century Origins," in Helmholz et al., *The Privilege against Self-Incrimination.*

77 **excesses were wholly secret.'"** R. H. Helmholz, "The Privilege and *Ius Commune*: The Middle Ages to the Seventeenth Century," in Helmholz et al., *The Privilege against Self-Incrimination,* 32–33.

77 **analogous to torture.** Albert W. Alschuler, "A Peculiar Privilege in Historical Perspective," in Helmholz et al., *The Privilege against Self-Incrimination,* 191.

78 as had been the case historically." Alschuler, "A Peculiar Privilege in Historical Perspective" (citing Levy), 430.

78 *State v. Hobbs* (1803), 2 *Tyl.* 380.

79 necessarily a right against torture," Levy, *Origins of the Fifth Amendment*, 326.

79 such Tortures as be Barborous and inhumane. Levy, *Origins of the Fifth Amendment*, 120–21.

80 a safeguard against torture." Alschuler, "A Peculiar Privilege in Historical Perspective," 185, 192 n61.

80 against the use of "judicial torture." Moglen, "The Privilege in British North America," 135.

80 exclusionary rule as its remedy. Professor Henry Smith has noted that the

> remedy for violation of the witness privilege was not exclusion.... The witness could raise the objection and might not be subject to contempt of court, but there is no evidence until several decades later that exclusion of the testimony from use in a subsequent proceeding against the witness was a consequence of a violation of the witness privilege.... The idea that exclusion would be a remedy was treated as a novelty in the 1847 *Garbett* case, suggesting strongly that the early-nineteenth-century witness privilege was not backed up by an exclusionary remedy. This is all the more striking since the confession rule, by contrast, was a "remedially" exclusionary rule that led to later exclusion of the confession obtained. ("The Modern Privilege: Its Nineteenth-Century Origins," 157)

81 himself *or any other person.*" Leonard MacNally, *The Rules of Evidence on Pleas of the Crown* (Dublin: H. Fitzpatrick, 1802), at 275 (emphasis added).

81 a right not to be tortured. A debate between George Nicholas and George Mason (who drafted the Virginia Bill of Rights) may also shed some light on the original understanding. Nicholas argued that the Bill of Rights "is but a paper check," which was frequently violated. *The Debates in the Several State Conventions on the Adoption of the Federal Constitution*, 446. He went on: "If we had no security against torture but our declaration of rights, we might be tortured to-morrow; for it has

been repeatedly infringed and disregarded" (451). Mason responded as follows: "The worthy gentleman was mistaken in his assertion that the bill of rights did not prohibit torture; for that one clause expressly provided that no man can given evidence against himself; and that the worthy gentleman must know that, in those countries where torture is used, evidence was extorted from the criminal himself" (452).

81 **vehicle for safeguarding against torture.** This was no different with regard to the due process clause of the Fourteenth Amendment or comparable provisions of state constitutions. As Levy writes: "No state, for example, had a due process of law clause in its own constitution, and only New York had recommended such a clause in place of the more familiar 'law of the land' clause" (*Origins of the Bill of Rights*, 248).

81 **the privilege against self-incrimination.** According to Levy, the historical connection between torture and "cruel" punishment is flimsy at best and not understood when looked at through modern eyes. See *Origins of the Bill of Rights*, 232–33.

82 **at issue in the case.** *Marbury v. Madison*, 5 U.S. 137 (1803).

82 **tend to criminate himself.'"** Levy, *Origins of the Fifth Amendment*, 429.

82 **without the assistance of counsel.** The witness in the *Marbury* case was, in fact, a lawyer. Indeed, he was "in the peculiar position of being both a witness and counsel for the government" in that case. Yet he had no obligation of disclosure because a truthful answer might incriminate him.

82 **greatest criminal trial in American history."** Albert J. Beveridge, *The Life of John Marshall* (Cambridge, MA: Riverside Press, 1919), 3:275. Another commentator notes:

> While under criminal indictment for the murder [of Alexander Hamilton, whom he killed in a duel] in New York and New Jersey, he had presided over the 1804 impeachment trial of Justice Samuel Chase. This had led one Federalist newspaper to quip that traditionally it was "the practice in Courts of Justice to arraign the *murderer* before the *Judge*, but now we behold the *Judge* arraigned before the *murderer*." (John C. Yoo, "The First Claim: The Burr Trial, United States v. Nixon, and Presidential Power," 83 *Minnesota Law Review* 1435 [1999], at 1439)

82   the answer might criminate himself." *U.S. v. Burr*, 25 Fed. Case. 38, no. 14, 692e C.C.D. Va. (1807).

83   **without referencing the Constitution.** Marshall did cite the Constitution in his opinion on whether the president could be subpoenaed, but interestingly, he cited the wrong amendment: "The eighth amendment to the Constitution gives to the accused, in all criminal prosecutions, a right to a speedy and public trial, and to compulsory process for obtaining witnesses in this favor" J. J. Coombs, *The Trial of Aaron Burr for High Treason* (Washington, DC: W. H. and O. H. Morrison, 1864) 43. It is the Sixth, not the Eighth Amendment, that accords those rights.

83   **through much of our history.** In *Boyd v. United States* 116 U.S. 630 (1886), the Court recognized that the Fourth and Fifth Amendments granted privacy rights from the production of incriminating documents.

83   **other questions not criminating himself."** Coombs, *The Trial of Aaron Burr*, 95–96.

84   **"conceal" a misdemeanor.** Misprision of felony was a crime, but misprision of misdemeanor may not have been—at least in Marshall's view. An encyclopedia published in 1881 states that "misprision of misdemeanor is unknown to the law." See John J. Lalor, *Cyclopoedia of Political Science, Political Economy, and the Political History of the United States by the Best American and European Writers* (New York: Maynard, Merrill, 1881), II.248.19, www.econlib.org/LIBRARY/YPDBooks/Lalor/llCy639.html.

85   **taken immediately into custody.** Leonard Levy, *Jefferson and Civil Liberties* (Chicago: Ivan R. Dee, 1989), 72.

86   **to avoid their recurrence.** See Dershowitz, *Rights from Wrongs*.

86   **expose him to a criminal charge."** *Ullmann v. U.S.* at 431.

87   **what the Fifth Amendment prohibits.** *Ullmann v. U.S.* at 450.

87   **were essentially correct.** There are numerous examples throughout early British and American history of the privilege being invoked against infamy. See, e.g., Levy, *Origins of the Bill of Rights*, 191. Professor Henry E. Smith seconds Levy's conclusion that the privilege applied to self-infamy, but discusses it in nineteenth-century England instead of eighteenth-century North America. See "The Modern Privilege," 157.

87   **on grounds of self-incrimination."** Levy, "The Right against Self-Incrimination: History and Judicial History," 23.

90 **"an unqualified prohibition of torture."** Albert W. Alschuler, "The Privilege and Common Law Criminal Procedure: The Sixteenth to the Eighteenth Centuries," in Helmholz et al., *The Privilege against Self-Incrimination*, 192.

91 **a defendant's subsequent criminal trial.** If the Constitution did prohibit torture, then judges were obliged by their oath of office not to permit it, even if the fruits were never introduced against a defendant. As Judge Chase wrote in the 1800 case *United States v. Callender*, "No position can be more clear than that all federal judges are bound by the solemn obligation of religion to regulate their decisions agreeably to Constitution of United States, and that it is standard of their determination in all cases that come before them." *United States v Callender* 25 F Cas 239 (1800).

91 **who posed security threats.** See Levy, *Origins of the Fifth Amendment*, 345.

91 **their dangerous confederates.** For a recounting of the Benthamite arguments, see Dershowitz, *Why Terrorism Works*, 131–63.

92 **"barbarous and inhumane"** This is somewhat reminiscent of the distinction made by the Bush administration. According to the *Washington Post*, under the direction of the vice president's office the administration has taken numerous steps to create a distinction between torture, which is forbidden, and the use of "cruel, inhuman, or degrading" methods of questioning, which are sometimes permitted.

CHAPTER 6

94 **against the weight of the state."** Erwin N. Griswold, *The Right to Be Let Alone*, 55 Northwestern University Law Review 216 (1960), at 221.

94 **enforcement of its criminal laws."** 493 U.S. 549 (1990), at 556.

95 **essence of modern democracy."** Telford Taylor, "The Constitutional Privilege against Self-Incrimination," *Annals of the American Academy of Political and Social Science* 300 (Jul. 1955): 116.

101 **or by state legislatures.** See Note, "The Bounds of Legislative Specification: A Suggested Approach to the Bill of Attainder Clause," 72 *Yale Law Journal*, no. 2 (Dec. 1962), at 330 n1.

103 **structural or symbolic reading.** See, e.g., *United States v. Lovett*, 328 U.S. 303 (1946), at 321, quoted in Note, "The Bounds of Legislative Specification," 341.

103 **views with which they disagree.** Alan Dershowitz, *Shouting Fire* (Boston: Little, Brown, 2002), 139–40.

105 **infringement by the government.** The Fourteenth Amendment issue proves something of a dilemma for some conservatives, such as former attorney general Edwin Meese, who do not believe that the Fourteenth Amendment applies the Bill of Rights to the states, but would like to interpret the Constitution as prohibiting state abridgment of the right to keep and bear arms.

105 **'rights' to exist at all."** Charlton Heston, speech to the National Press Club, 11 Feb. 1997.

105 **with the narrow interpretation.** See Amar, *America's Constitution*, 323.

105 **applies only in criminal trials.** See *United States v. Salerno*.

106 **prohibition against government abuse.** *Ingraham v. Wright*, 430 U.S. 651 (1977), at 664.

106 **Fifteenth, and Nineteenth Amendments.** See, e.g., Akhil Reed Amar, *The Bill of Rights: Creation and Reconstruction* (New Haven: Yale University Press, 1998), 114–15; Levy, *Origins of the Fifth Amendment*, 239–40; Akhil Amar, *The Bill of Rights: Creation and Reconstruction*, 124–25.

107 **aspire after future ones.** Antonin Scalia, *A Matter of Interpretation* (Princeton: Princeton University Press, 1997), 134–35.

109 **a static constitutional law.** Eben Moglen, "The Privilege and Common Law Criminal Procedure: The Sixteenth to the Eighteenth Centuries," in Helmholz et al., *The Privilege against Self-Incrimination*, 129.

110 **endless, perpetual posterity."** Calvin Colton, *The Life, Correspondence, and Speeches of Henry Clay in Six Volumes* (New York: A. S. Barnes & Co., 1857), 344.

111 **That day.** No. 1212 (c. 1872).

113 **various crises of human affairs."** *McCulloch v. Maryland*, 17 U.S. 316 (1819).

113 **unavailable at the founding."** Donald Dripps, "Akhil Amar on Criminal Procedure and Constitutional Law: 'Here I Go Down That Wrong Road Again,'" 74 *North Carolina Law Review* 1559 (1996), at 1625.

114 **that they did not envision.** A teleological argument could be made that by including the right to counsel and the right to call witnesses in the Sixth Amendment, the framers laid the foundation for a criminal justice system in which the lawyer would speak and the

defendant, with the advice of his lawyer, would decide whether to testify in his own behalf. But this argument sounds like the kind of "just so" stories often told to explain why the leopard has spots or why the snake walks on its belly. Stephen Jay Gould, "Not Necessarily a Wing," *Natural History* 94 (Oct. 1985): 12–19.

115 **have fallen largely on deaf ears.** But see *Griswold v. Connecticut*, where the Supreme Court referred to the Third Amendment as "another facet of that privacy": "Various guarantees create zones of privacy. The right of association contained in the penumbra of the First Amendment is one, as we have seen. The Third Amendment in its prohibition against the quartering of soldiers 'in any house' in time of peace without the consent of the owner is another facet of that privacy." *Griswold v. Connecticut*, 381 U.S. 479 (1965), at 484.

115 **"right to bear arms."** "Bear arms" had a rather technical meaning at the Founding, referring to a military context. Soldiers bore arms. Hunters carried rifles.

CHAPTER 7

117 **termed 'historical functionalism.'"** "The Bounds of Legislative Specification: A Suggested Approach to the Bill of Attainder Clause," *Yale Law Journal* 72, no. 2 (Dec. 1962), at 333 n20.

118 **application of the exclusionary rule.** *Hudson v. Michigan*, 126 S. Ct. 2159 (2006).

119 **informed the decision in Martinez.** In *Kyllo v. United States*, 533 U.S. 27 (2001), Justice Scalia authored a majority opinion that disallowed law enforcement's use of a thermal sensoring device in a home without a warrant. He said, "The Fourth Amendment is to be construed in the light of what was deemed an unreasonable search and seizure when it was adopted."

119 **anything to stop being tortured.** For examples of torture producing self-proving, truthful intelligence, see the 1995 case in which Philippine authorities tortured a terror suspect into divulging information that may have foiled plots to assassinate the pope, crash eleven commercial airliners into the ocean, and fly an explosive-filled Cessna aircraft into CIA headquarters, discussed in Alan Dershowitz, *Why Terrorism Works* (New Haven, CT: Yale University Press, 2002), 137; *Leon v.*

Wainwright (734 F.2d 770, 1984), a case in which the Miami police choked a suspect "until he revealed where [a kidnapping victim] was being held"; the use of torture against the French Resistance, which produced the locations of other resistance members, discussed in Alan Dershowitz, "Democrats and Waterboarding," *The Wall Street Journal*, 7 Nov. 2007.

121   **searching a home or a computer.** See Alan M. Dershowitz, *Preemption* (New York: Norton, 2006), 5, citing Cass Sunstein, *Laws of Fear: Beyond the Precautionary Principle* (New York: Cambridge University Press, 2005), 4, 13, 15.

CHAPTER 8

128   **proper mode or modes of interpretation.** See, e.g., "Advisory Opinion, Consistency of Certain Danzig Legislative Decrees with the Constitution of the Free City," in Richard Donnelly, Joseph Goldstein, and Richard Schwartz, eds., *Criminal Law* (New York: Free Press, 1962), 885.

129   ***Brown v. Board of Education*** (1954). See, e.g., Christopher Shea, "Supreme Downsizing," *Boston Globe*, 7 Oct. 2007, E1–2.

129   **this wasn't always the case)** See Herbert Wechsler, "Toward Neutral Principles of Constitutional Law," 73 *Harvard Law Review* 1 (1959), at 26–35.

130   **not what I want to impose on the society."** Quoted in Alan Dershowitz, *Supreme Injustice* (Oxford: Oxford University Press, 2001), 131. In a letter written in 1801, Thomas Jefferson railed against "the conscience of the judge" becoming the "umpire" of freedom of speech. See Alan Dershowitz, *Finding Jefferson* (Hoboken, NJ: John Wiley & Sons, 2008), 197.

131   **subject to reasonable restrictions and limitations.** A similar debate is under way with regard to torture. See Sanford Levinson, ed., *Torture: A Collection* (Oxford: Oxford University Press, 2004). For a brilliant defense of Justice Black's tactic of absolutes, see Charles L. Black, Jr., "Mr. Justice Black, the Supreme Court, and Bill of Rights," *Harper's Magazine* (Feb. 1961): 63–68. Interestingly, Charles Black acknowledges the impossibility of sticking with absolutes under all circumstances, using a prescient example relevant to this book:

> No right, however defined, ever turns out to be really "absolute,"
> if you think about it long enough. Take torture. General

immunity from being tortured is something all of us would regard as an essential of civilized life. We might carelessly refer to it as an "absolute." But what if an atom bomb were ticking somewhere in the city, and the roads were closed and the trains were not running, and the man who knew where the bomb was hidden sat grinning and silent in a chair at the country police station twenty miles away? Could the "absolute right" not to be tortured really prevail?

132　**expanding view of constitutional rights.** "Our Constitution, unlike some others, strikes the balance in favor of the right of the accused to be advised by his lawyer of his privilege against self-incrimination." *Escobedo v. Illinois*, 378 U.S. 478 (1964), at 488.

133　**a time long past.**" *Michael H. v. Gerald D.*, 491 U.S. 110 (1989), at 141 (Brennan, W., dissenting).

133　**changes of social circumstance.** William J. Brennan, "The Constitution of the United States: Contemporary Ratification," lecture presented at the Text and Teaching Symposium, Georgetown University, Washington, DC, 12 Oct. 1985, www.fed-soc.org/resources/id.50/default.asp.

133　**liberty, equality, due process.** It is difficult to justify a "living" constitution that does not also contract when circumstances warrant. See Dershowitz, *Rights from Wrongs*, 225-31.

134　**a narrowing of constitutional rights.** This has not always been the case. When legislatures were more progressive than courts, liberal justices, such as Louis Brandeis, favored a narrow view of the judicial function.

135　**our most essential tool.** Aharon Barak, "A Judge on Judging: The Role of a Supreme Court in a Democracy," 116 *Harvard Law Review* 16 (Nov. 2002), at 81-82.

CONCLUSION

138　**jurisprudence to fill that gap.** See Dershowitz, *Preemption*, 237.

139　**its abolition or limitation.** See, e.g., Henry J. Friendly, "The Fifth Amendment Tomorrow: The Case for Constitutional Change," 37 *University of Cincinnati Law Review*, no. 4 (1968).

141   to produce a "just" outcome. See Alan Dershowitz, *The Best Defense* (New York: Random House, 1982), 150–51.

141   probable guilt or innocence. See Henry J. Friendly, "Is Innocence Irrelevant? Collateral Attack on Criminal Judgments," 38 *University of Chicago Law Review*, no. 1 (autumn 1970): 142–72.

144   assessment of the self-incrimination clause. See Akhil R. Amar, *The Constitution and Criminal Procedure* (New Haven: Yale University Press, 1997), 46–89.

149   not the Fourth Amendment. Levy writes about Jefferson's view of torture in *Origins of the Fifth Amendment*: "Jefferson would have included a ban on legislative prescription of torture, but he neglected a ban against compulsory self-incrimination" (408).

149   the New York courts. See Levy, *Origins of the Fifth Amendment*, 424–25.

149   expressed more gratefully elsewhere, See Alan M. Dershowitz, "Crime and Truth," *Slate*, 26 Mar. 1997, www.slate.com/id/ 2972.

151   he happened to find together.' Dershowitz, *Rights from Wrongs*, 43.

153   credibility, demeanor, and responsiveness. See Dershowitz, *Reasonable Doubts*.

154   (and even more by civil litigants). Alan Dershowitz, "Legal Ethics Symposium: Lawyers' Ethics in an Adversary System: Legal Ethics and the Constitution," 34 *Hofstra Law Review* 747 (spring 2006).

157   in the absence of legislative authorization. See *Murphy v. Waterfront*, which held that "a state witness granted immunity from prosecution under state law may not be compelled to give testimony which may incriminate him under federal law unless such testimony and its fruits cannot be used in connection with a federal prosecution against him" but "with the removal of the fear of federal prosecution, the petitioners may be compelled to answer."

157   a witness's right against self-incrimination. Amar, *The Constitution and Criminal Procedure*, 49.

160   the more general concept of due process. See *Brown v. Mississippi*, 297 U.S. 278 (1936).

163   confessions in the courtroom. Judges too often go through charades in accepting guilty pleas that border on suborning perjury. For

example, they often ask the defendant whether his lawyer has made any "predictions" as to the sentence that will be imposed. The negative answer that is expected is almost always a lie, since lawyers generally offer such predictions, based on guideline calculations and knowledge of the judge's sentencing practices.

164 **many white deaths as well.** See Dershowitz, *America Declares Independence*, 125; "Jefferson on the Missouri Question and Slavery to John Holmes April 22, 1820," in Paul Leicester Ford, ed., *The Works of Thomas Jefferson*, Vol. 12 (New York: Putnam, 1905), 159. "We have the wolf by the ears and feel the danger of either holding or letting him loose" (Jefferson to Mrs. Sigourney, Monticello, 18 July 1824).

165 **that do not have a right against self-incrimination).** Criminal lawyers in the United States (at least good ones) become involved in a proactive way at a far earlier point than their continental counterparts. Indeed, what American lawyers routinely do—and are often required to by ethical rules and guidelines—would constitute an obstruction of justice in some European countries. See George P. Fletcher and Steve Sheppard, *American Law in a Global Context: The Basics* (Oxford: Oxford University Press, 2005).

166 **answer would be "yes."** See *Brogan v. United States*, 522 U.S. 398 (1998).

166 **does not expose himself to criminal prosecution.** See Gordon Van Kessel, "Adversary Excesses in the American Criminal Trial," 67 *Notre Dame Law Review* 403 (1992), at 480.

168 **far more complex than that.** Another difference between our system of criminal justice and most continental and other Western systems is the fact that in many of our states, prosecutors and judges are elected, and where not elected are appointed on a political basis. Being a prosecutor is an important stepping-stone to higher office. Moreover, the criminal justice system has become the subject of partisan political campaigns in which candidates—for virtually every office—vie over who is tougher on crime. This politicization of criminal justice often changes the role of prosecutor from a neutral, almost magistrate-type justice-doer to a zealous advocate with a political agenda. This alone may not justify a vibrant right against self-incrimination, but neither can it be ignored in assessing the arguments for its abolition or significant curtailment.

169   in the Fourth Amendment context, See *Illinois v. Caballes*, 543 U.S. 405 (2005).

171   as steps leading to trial. For example, in *Cox v. Louisiana*, 379 U.S. 559 (1965), at 566, Justice Goldberg wrote that "an arrest...is normally the first step in a series of legal proceedings."

171   history of the common law. See Dershowitz, "Preventive Confinement: A Suggested Framework for Constitutional Analysis," *Texas Law Review* 51, no. 7 (Nov. 1973): 1277-1324.

173   related mechanisms of social control. Taken to its logical conclusion, this "reasoning" could lead to an absurd ruling that therapeutic execution of the kind carried out in Nazi Germany was not "punishment" because the legislative purpose was eugenic and preventive.

174   in an ad hoc manner. See *Seling v. Young*, 531 U.S. 250 (U.S. 2001); *Kan. v. Hendricks*, 521 U.S. 346 (U.S. 1997); *Hamdan v. Rumsfeld*, 126 S. Ct. 2749 (U.S. 2006); *Rasul v. Bush*, 542 U.S. 466 (U.S. 2004); *Hamdi v. Rumsfeld*, 542 U.S. 507 (U.S. 2004).

174   information at subsequent criminal trials. Alan Dershowitz, "A Stick with Two Ends," *Opening Argument* (Yale Law School), Feb. 2006, http://openingargument.com/index.php?name=Home&file=arti-article&did=68. See also Alan Dershowitz, "The Greatest Threat to Civil Liberties Would Be Another Atrocity Like 9/11," *Spectator* (UK), 2 Sept. 2006, 12.

175   abusively coercive interrogations. Another abusive tactic that some prosecutors currently employ is to spring a "perjury trap" on a witness who has been immunized. This tactic—which is reminiscent of the oath *ex officio*—involves subpoenaing a witness to testify in a manner that exposes him to a perjury charge. It raises the following important question: Can an unimmunized witness properly invoke the Fifth Amendment in answer to an incriminating question when a truthful answer would be substantively exculpatory, but he reasonably fears that the prosecution would disbelieve his answer and use it as a basis for indicting him for perjury? It seems like a simple question. Of course he can invoke the privilege, since his answer would provide a link in the chain of incrimination. Indeed, it would be the crucial link—the *actus reus* of the crime itself. Yet if the answer to that question is yes, then it

throws into doubt the entire concept of derivative use immunity (or even of transactional immunity), at least in that context. Here is why. If a witness is given immunity, he must then answer all questions truthfully. If he does not, he can be indicted for perjury. He cannot refuse to answer an incriminating question on the ground that a truthful answer would expose him to a perjury prosecution, since it is well established that immunity does not protect against perjury.

This is the situation that Roger Clemens might have faced, had he chosen to plead the Fifth before the Congressional Committee. (See Dershowitz, "Why Roger Clemens, Even if Innocent, Should Take the Fifth," *Huffington Post*, 11 Jan. 2008.) He could then have been given immunity and be compelled to answer. Let us assume that the truth is that he never took banned substances. But let us also assume that if he had testified to that effect, he risked being indicted for perjury, since another witness said he did. A person in Clemens's situation should be entitled to invoke the Fifth, even after being given immunity, but he probably would not be allowed to do so.

If it is true that an unimmunized witness can invoke the Fifth out of fear that a truthful exculpatory answer might expose him to perjury, then it would seem to follow logically that immunity is simply not coterminous with the privilege, at least in that situation.

176   **harmful conduct, such as terrorism.** Other harmful actions that are currently subject to preventive state action are sexual predation, environmental destruction, and corporate abuses. See Paul Robinson, "Punishing Dangerous: Cloaking Preventive Detention as Criminal Justice," 114 *Harvard Law Review* 1429 (Mar. 2001), at 1429; Alan Dershowitz, "The Origins of Preventive Confinement in Anglo-American Law," 43 *University of Cincinnati Law Review* 781 (1974). Preventive state action can also take the form of mandated disclosure and regulation. Federal bodies such as the Environmental Protection Agency and the Occupational Safety and Health Administration preventively regulate and monitor the activities of industry. Likewise, laws have been put in place—such as the Sarbanes-Oxley Act of 2002 (107 P.L. 204)—that mandate disclosure of public corporations' finances in order to prevent corporate abuses.

Index

. . .

INDEX

Miranda warnings (*continued*)
 Court opinions on, 8, 9; and suspect's
 privilege, 160
misdemeanors, concealing, 84, 195
Moglen, Eben, 109
Morgan, Edmund, M, 139
Murphy v. Waterfront Commission (1964),
 41–42, 56, 95, 97, 186–87; and
 derivative use immunity, 157, 200

National Rifle Association, 105
Nicholas, George, 193–94
9/11, xii, 20, 138
Nineteenth Amendment, 106
Ninth Amendment, 106
North, Oliver, 159

oaths *ex officio*: framers' fears of, 150; and
 general warrants, 190; as weapon
 against dissidents, 65–66, 69, 73–74,
 89
O'Connor, Sandra Day, 12, 13
originalist approach, 129
original understanding: in *Chavez v.*
 Martinez, 33, 34, 54, 89, 92, 135; in
 constitutional interpretation, viii–ix,
 26–28, 33–37, 127; functional analysis
 and, 118; Marshall opinions as source
 for, 81–85, 90; Scalia's misuse of, 109,
 111–12; of self-incrimination clause,
 viii–ix, 28–30, 33–37, 88–90, 127; on
 torture, 89, 90–92, 193–94
Origins of the Fifth Amendment (Levy),
 6, 64

Palko v. Connecticut (1937), 94
perjury: in coercion hearings, 188; and
 evidentiary privileges, 154–55; in
 hybrid justice system, 166–67; and
 judges' tactics, 201; and *Miranda*
 warnings, 9; as part of "cruel trilemma,"
 7, 166, 167
Pillsbury Co. v. Conboy, 50, 51

point of impact: in *Chavez v. Martinez*, 19,
 31, 51, 53; in *Murphy v. Waterfront*
 Commission, 42
police interrogation: cultural
 representations of, 159; station house,
 146; and suspect's privilege, 75–76;
 tactics, 162–63. *See also* coercion
policy analysis approach, 117–18, 128
political dissent: Fifth Amendment
 origins in, 55, 64–68; First Amendment
 origins in, 140–41; in McCarthy era, 75,
 76; and unknown crimes, 73–74
Pound, Roscoe, 139
precedent, in *Chavez v. Martinez*, 40–53,
 135
press, free, clause, 104
presumption of innocence, xiii, 88, 105,
 153, 165, 169
pretrial detention, 27, 169, 172–73, 188
preventive intelligence: and CIA methods,
 179; historical, 64, 91; moral and legal
 questions in, 120–22. *See also* torture
preventive state: after 9/11, xii, 20, 138;
 focus of, viii, xii, 19, 20, 137–38, 171,
 202–3; lack of jurisprudence for,
 xiii–xiv, 170–76; police in, 171;
 potential abuses in, 6, 19–20, 24,
 137–38, 146, 163, 169
privacy: rights, 140–41, 169, 195, 198;
 Supreme Court opinions on, 95–96; and
 Third Amendment, 115
privilege against self-incrimination.
 See self-incrimination clause
privileges, evidentiary. *See* evidentiary
 privileges
punishment, as social control, 172–73, 202

reactive (deterrent) state: criminal justice
 system under, 170–71; objectives of,
 viii; shift away from, xiii, 19, 137
Rehnquist, William, xi, 12, 13, 172
religious dissent: Fifth Amendment
 origins in, 55, 64–68; First Amendment
 origins in, 140–41; and unknown
 crimes, 73–74

[210]